Sober Identity

Tools for Reprogramming the Addictive Mind

Lisa Neumann

BALBOA.
PRESS

A DIVISION OF HAY HOUSE

Balboa Press books may be ordered through booksellers or by contacting:

Balboa Press
A Division of Hay House
1663 Liberty Drive
Bloomington, IN 47403
www.balboapress.com
1-(877) 407-4847

ISBN: 978-1-4525-3919-5 (sc)
ISBN: 978-1-4525-3918-8 (hc)
ISBN: 978-1-4525-3920-1 (e)

Library of Congress Control Number: 2011915863

Because of the dynamic nature of the Internet, any web addresses or links contained in this book may have changed since publication and may no longer be valid. The views expressed in this work are solely those of the author and do not necessarily reflect the views of the publisher, and the publisher hereby disclaims any responsibility for them.

The author of this book does not dispense medical advice or prescribe the use of any technique as a form of treatment for physical, emotional, or medical problems without the advice of a physician, either directly or indirectly. The intent of the author is only to offer information of a general nature to help you in your quest for emotional and spiritual well-being. In the event you use any of the information in this book for yourself, which is your constitutional right, the author and the publisher assume no responsibility for your actions.

Any people depicted in stock imagery provided by Thinkstock are models, and such images are being used for illustrative purposes only. Certain stock imagery © Thinkstock.

Printed in the United States of America

Balboa Press rev. date: 10/11/2011

For my dad and mom

CONTENTS

Preface

The pursuit of this work has ultimately one purpose: for the reader to receive the awareness of what is possible. This book has been written, ideally, for the individual who longs for sobriety yet has difficulty acting in accordance with this (sometimes fleeting) desire. This book shares the path of this addict's recovery. This work is the achievement and maintenance of a life free of mind-altering substances. Use it as one resource among many that are available. It provides a road map to accomplishing a sober life—a sober identity.

The seed of hope is necessary for change to occur. Without the possibility of an alternative future, we are barricaded, chained to our pasts. From this prison, addicts find no real reason to change. Why would we want to? The future looks like more of the same—failed attempts. It is not a coincidence that people who achieve are those who believe that they *can* achieve. Moving into the mind-set of achievement will be a chief aim of this book. Failure is no longer an option!

While not thrilled with the stigma of being a recovered alcoholic, it is fair to say I am now grateful that I saw the truth of my lies. My ability to be willing to do life differently from what I had ever done before was, ultimately, what saved my life. My thoughts mirrored my world. Once receptive to developing the quality of my *thinking*, the quality of my *life* changed—substantially.

This is the story of my recovery from alcohol and other mind-altering drugs. What did I recover from? The panic that arose when alcohol was not present; the anxiety of awaiting the first drink; the debilitation while wondering if there was more to fill my glass; the false moment of ecstasy that came with the first cocktail; the way I chased that false moment for

1

the remainder of the evening despite the fact that I couldn't repeat it; the certainty that I could do nothing unless I was drinking or drugging; the living regretfully and forgetting so many moments that had passed. Yes, I have recovered.

I had many influences and resources throughout my recovery. The twelve-step program is one of these resources. While I do not address the twelve-step model within the context of this book, I am a proponent of the twelve-step program. The application of the twelve-step program will set a strong foundation for lasting sobriety. For me, twelve steps, and then some, were required. This work is my journey, my recovery from alcoholism and addiction.

Included within the text are ten challenges that coincide with the materials discussed. When implemented, these challenges will help redirect your thinking and thus your life. That is their purpose.

I remain compelled to evolve as I grow away from my last drink; as such, the seeming complexity of lasting sobriety is the solution presented here. Lasting sobriety seems so complex because it is so challenging for so many. It need not be. We think we need to learn a lot of new stuff. We do not. What is required is an unlearning of nonfunctional perceptions and inherited beliefs. These are the concepts and principles that changed my life, all because of the seed of hope that life—that I—could be different.

We can change our lives if that is what we choose. It is a choice. We decide—nobody else.

Introduction

Just because we don't like that we are addicted is of little importance. Liking the situation or not is a luxury of thought that we are not granted. Not liking or even abhorring this fact will not change it. Beliefs are different from truths. Just because we don't believe we are addicted does not make it true. The truth always stands on its own, despite our beliefs about it. Truth isn't subjective, nor is it determined by how many people believe it. Truth just is. Whether we have had glimpses of or been blindsided by our addictions, their existence is no more or less the truth.

The purpose of this book is to give the reader a greater understanding of how to live a fulfilled life, one without drinking or drugging. It is for people who want to be proactive in their recovery from alcohol, from addiction.

It is not the purpose of this book to define what alcoholism is or whether or not one is an alcoholic. If we are not sure whether or not we are alcoholics, the hope is that we will be receptive to hearing the truth.

Nor is it my objective to define whether or not alcoholism is a disease. The road to sobriety is not determined by identifying this information. *Disease* can be an ambiguous word, anyway. The origins of the word disease are rooted in *dis*—meaning "to be without or apart" and—*ease* meaning "comfort." In this sense, all humans experience disease. It seems a condition of human nature. For many alcoholics and addicts, the disease mentality can serve as a hindrance to recovery, as people use it as an acceptable excuse for repetitive and harmful actions. Recovery is the same for every alcoholic or addict. There is no way around this. Abstinence is the required condition. Without it, little else can develop.

How to achieve a state of abstinence is the issue addressed within these pages. The actual time it takes to make a decision is only an instant. Once the decision has been made and the ties severed, "using" no longer remains an option—one simply stops finding ways to make the using work. And once the old has been dismissed, there is space for something new to enter.

We are so afraid of who we will be if we are sober. The work involved in abstaining seems too great. We don't yet understand who we will become, and the dilemma of letting go of the familiar is paralyzing. Abstinence seems the oddest and harshest of options; we would prefer to maintain our lives, despite the obvious problems our addictions are causing. We see anyone's attempt at helping us get sober as a plot to control us. We preserve our right to drink or drug at the peril of self and all around us. And so we are partnered with this puzzling desire—a desire we wish we did not have.

We think that giving in to someone else's way means that we are weak, that admitting we have a problem means we can't control our own lives. So we pretend that we know what we are doing. We pretend to have it under control. We pretend and lie and believe our lie, and if we believe our lie long enough, somehow that will make it true. This will never make it true! *We are far from what is true when we are drinking and drugging.* When we are open to hearing the power of these words, we are well on our way to that moment in our lives when everything begins to change—that moment in time when we achieve a state of abstinence. This moment can and will last a lifetime, if we let it.

If we want something new in our lives, we prepare to do something new to acquire it. This is the simplest of solutions to our predicament. The difference between us and the people who have what we say we want is that they don't accept the excuses that we do for not having it. We prefer to want-to-want something. This way, we don't have to put forth much effort, and if we fail, we figure we didn't want it that much in the first place. When juggling the idea of sobriety, most of us want a promise that our actions will be worth the exerted effort. Not only do we want our efforts to be rewarding, we want the reward with the minimum exertion put forth. Suffice it to say, we don't want to do the work unless someone is going to give us a signed guarantee on the exact payoff. No one can give us that kind of assurance. Our free will is always a factor in the equation. Only we have that answer. What *can* be promised is that living a principled, spiritual, and conscientious life will keep us sober: principled in order that we may adhere to universal guidelines; spiritual because something greater than us created us; conscientious to continuously grow into a greater understanding of whom we are becoming.

If we are unhappy now (sober or not sober), what we have is a thriving set of beliefs that are holding us down. Not only are they holding us down, they are feeding our neurosis. Our minds are telling us, convincing us, working overtime to prove this point: *this is as good as it gets.* It says: we don't deserve anything more or better; we tried and it didn't work; we're not enough the way we are; we can't do it as good as they can; that's good for them, but not for us; it's too difficult, costs too much, will take too much time; and—most especially—change is not necessary. Whatever garbage we hear (and by "garbage" I mean the stuff that pulls us down), it's a pre-recorded program that's ruling our life. And, regardless of how it got there, it's all unquestioned thought. Rather, it's a memory in the mind that we seek to fulfill, because no one ever taught us that we don't have to listen to every crazy thought we have. We've never comprehended how much more was possible—so we've settled for much less. A happy, fulfilled, sober life is not an oxymoron. It's a fact for many people.

At the writing of this, I consider myself a fully recovered alcoholic. Recovered from what? I'm recovered from the thought that I must drink to be happy, to be interesting, to be a comfortable, confident me. I'm recovered from the need to drink or do drugs on a daily basis so that I can function. I'm recovered from the paramount and incessant desire to purchase and ingest drugs and alcohol. I'm recovered from living a conceited, contemptuous life. I'm recovered from the idea that I am alone in this world and that no one understands or is capable of understanding how I feel. I'm recovered from thinking mostly about myself—arrogantly. I'm recovered from the idea that my feelings, if felt, will kill me. I'm recovered from the concept that I am a hostage in my own body. I am recovered, and I believe I will continue to be recovered, because I have learned the necessities of acquiring and maintaining sobriety on any given day.

Lasting sobriety is achieved within the mind-set of abstaining from alcohol and drugs. Our ability to abstain is the by-product, at first, of sheer desperation—the waking nightmare of our lives. Over time, however, we grow to enjoy the waking hours. It is then that recovery takes on a momentum of its own—abstinence becomes normal. As long as we stay in alignment with this momentum, we stay sober. When we veer, the impetus is compromised, and once compromised, it becomes difficult to regain our drive—difficult, but doable. One failed attempt at earnest sobriety can set the pattern for sobriety that does not last. The stakes get higher, we get sicker, and the target seems farther and farther away with every abandoned attempt.

The key is to see that getting sober is never ever going to be pain-free for any real addict. But we reject this idea. We want it to be painless. It is not. The best we can do is walk in with our eyes wide open and suck it up for a while. The moment for sobriety is right now. It will never become easier than it is at this moment—never! And if this statement frightens us, we can be 99.99 percent certain we have an addiction problem.

There are six main parts to this book: the Observation, the Process, the Essentials, the Competencies, the Partnership, and the Basics. Included within these parts are the Dialogues.

Part I: The Observation

Before anything can change, one must first become aware of what needs changing. As a general rule, most addicts believe that if we could just stop or curtail our addiction, our life would be fine. We believe that the alcohol or drugs are the problem. It never rightly strikes our mind that we succumb to this craving because we can't cope with reality. Our addiction to drugs or alcohol is the end result, not the problem itself. The very thing we need to change is ourself. Our inability to accurately identify the problem interferes with a workable solution. We place the blame outside of self. We expect others to be what we determine—then we can be happy. When they don't or can't (and sometimes even when they do), we use it as an excuse to drink.

Being honest about our inability to cope with an unaltered life is a confrontational yet required awareness. Without honest observation of our behavior, no workable solution will appear. There will, however, be plenty of solutions, just none that solve the infinite predicaments we face. We hide by misidentifying the exact problem. Exactly why we don't stay sober and how we manipulate our minds is the knowledge we will strive to understand.

Part II: The Process

The exact process of any type of work is always different, yet the end goal is the same: to achieve success. We take on the process to achieve the desired result. To do this, we must grow. We can't be where we are and somewhere else at the same time. If we're in a place we don't like, we don't have to remain there. We only have to genuinely want to be in a different place. That's it; that's the criterion. Without clarification on what we *don't* want, how will we ever know what we *do* want? We won't. We'll always get sucked into that first thought because we never learned how to move toward and act upon a second thought.

This book is about actual work, about looking at how we see the world at a conscious as well as a subconscious level. Until we are ready to actually do some work, we will be dissatisfied with our lives. Life is happening whether we like it or not. We can either go along with it and make it easy or fight it and get pulled. The choice is ours. I use this phrase "the choice is ours" with thoughtfulness. Until we recognize that there is another choice, we truly are hostage to our subconscious mind. However, upon reading these words, we have been injected with the thought, the idea, that there *can* be a different way. We can no longer say we don't know—now we know.

The process of recovery is both a structured and creative journey: structured because we need a standard, a model to follow to help guide our movement, and creative because we all start in different places and aim for different achievements. No two journeys are identical, because no two people are identical—only similar. We do not compare our progress and vision to another. The similarity we share is our desire for freedom. We learn to live free of alcohol and drugs, and in doing so, we learn to trust ourselves again. We must give this freedom a chance to work before we quit. After all, we've walked away before; this can be the time we stay. If we do walk away from this meeting point, we will be armed with very little to help us sustain anything new, and certainly not anything lasting. We are encouraged to stay. For now, we learn to trust the process.

Part III: The Essentials

As in nature, there is always a balance. Life shows up with the tide's rhythm, the Earth's seasons, and the certainty of the sun's rise. When we see our environment as the problem, we are in conflict with the apparent order of things. When we see the environment as the solution, we get ourself into that environment quickly. The goal is to flourish, not die.

We will explore science and gain knowledge of what our thoughts actually are—energy. We will learn what to do with energy we don't want and how to reprogram ourself with new energy.

Part IV: The Competencies

When we begin to develop and grow some key competencies, we will see a new balance in our lives, a balance that has previously not existed. Instead of focusing solely on our goal of staying sober, we will keep the focus on developing our competency. What do we spend the most time thinking about? Our answer to this question is the indicator of what has become most important in our lives. This is where our priorities lie. Our action, or lack of it, shows us what is most relevant at any given moment. Our actions are the greatest indicator of our sense of importance. Where do we spend our time? What consumes our money? For many, we do not like what we see. In our quest for alcohol or drugs, we have valued secrecy, omission, lying, and manipulation. We have spent money when we had none. We have taken from others what was not ours to take. This has been the quality of our thinking. We have been in an environment, both physical and emotional, that has not served us well. We must change our environment and begin to create a more manageable balance if we are to exist.

Part V: The Partnership

We have always been in partnership with something. That something is our *self*. We are the only person who listens and responds to the silent commentary in our head. We've been in a conversation with ourself since we were small. Only we have heard all the words that our mind has silently uttered—our private, speechless dialogue. The moment we awaken, the dialogue begins. *Get out of bed. No, just a few more minutes.* Then we hit the snooze button. If we are alone, who are those two voices talking? Plainly put, both voices are us. The voice we choose to listen to is the action that prevails. It's that simple.

Would we like to identify the voices in our head and decipher who is saying what and to whom? Yes, and we can learn to gather our thoughts with certainty. We can acquire the skill of deducing which voice is the one that is serving us best. After all, they both sound like us. The voice that wins is the one we feed. Not only will we learn to listen to self with objectivity, but we will discover how to listen to others with the same discerning, open perspective. All of this will help us to comprehend the voice of truth in our own head.

Natural laws or principles are the guidelines we are willing to honor as we live together on this planet. Individual principles are the philosophy out of which we govern our life. This means we act in accordance with our particular set of beliefs while extending this courtesy to others. Principles are the fundamental ethics we choose to live by in our everyday lives. Identifying our principles and philosophy is essential for our new identity to evolve. If we are feeling that our life is out of balance, then it is; and it is because we have not defined our principles or philosophy as they pertain to us. This lack of investigation and clarity has, in part, created and perpetuated our addicted and misguided lives. We've functioned in an unaware existence. We are unacquainted with self and thus are unaware of what's around us.

There are many influences in our environment. Our subconscious mind determines which ones get our attention. This data arrives from more than one path. As we explore this personal partnership more deeply, we will understand the science behind this partnership. We live in an unbelievably wise and wonderful universe; one that is here to support us in our endeavors. Welcome to life. We are about to see ourselves in a brand new way.

Part VI: The Basics

The bottom line here is work—hard work, conscious work, daily work, consistent work—and a no-quitting type of attitude. Stop thinking this should be totally comfortable all the time. It's not going to be, at least not for a little while. For most of the early days of sobriety, it is going to resemble an abyss; a deeper sinking into an unknown darkness. Stop expecting it to feel safe or good or freeing. Those are the rewards of the journey. They are not the journey itself.

We may hate this work at the onset, and then we will love it, and then we will hate it again, and then love it again. And this is the way of it. This is the way of life. The moment we understand that a perfect, issue-free life will never arrive, we are both thrilled and saddened—thrilled to know that we can stop trying so hard to create something that will never arrive (and if it does, it will be temporary), and saddened to think that we have spent a lifetime chasing something that was so fleeting. That being said, either everything is perfect or nothing is perfect. Either way, they mean the same thing. We have come to understand that everything happens for a reason, whether we comprehend it or not. We give situations their meaning, not the other way around. In this sense, things are perfectly imperfect. The imperfectly perfect moment is right now. And we know how to live in the now—finally!

The goal is to live happy, peaceful, and sober, to have a sober identity we are thrilled to have. One that is extraordinary because it's extraordinary to us. We cannot *give* each other our experiences; we can only *share* them. We get to create our own experiences. The journey is to find what works best for us and to not give up until we do.

The Dialogues

In total, there are seven sections of dialogues throughout the text that represent my internal conversations. Voice "A" is my lower self that represents love's opposite. It is my identity that is questioning, struggling, and is easily confused and/or angered by life on life's terms. Voice "B" is my higher self, my identity as experienced through the eyes of my Creator. Voice "B" is always the voice and choice for love at its highest level. Together, they represent my progression from pre-sobriety to recovery. The first dialogues reflect my internal war, the way I spoke most frequently to myself before I got sober and during my first year of sobriety. The middle dialogues represent my continued struggle to listen to and trust Voice "B." The last dialogues begin to show the harmony that is attainable when living in accordance with my own principles and philosophy. These thoughts echo the internal as well as the external quality of my life.

An important note to the reader:

The words *alcoholic* and *addict* are used interchangeably, as are the words *alcohol* and *drugs*. You, the reader, are encouraged to see how the situation pertains to you, foregoing attachment to the noun that is used. Many alcoholics consider themselves addicts, while others do not. Alcohol is a drug. We ingest it intending and expecting to alter our consciousness. Most addicts, if not familiar with alcohol, do not consider themselves alcoholics. There appears to be a subculture of drug addicts who have yet to experience alcoholism. Both alcohol and drugs are harmful addictions. Seeing how this information can help rather than hinder your life will be your best chance at sobriety. As they say in Alcoholics Anonymous, "Look for the similarities, not the differences." For anyone trying to achieve freedom from his or her addiction, cooperation rather than distinction and separateness serves the greatest good. In short, surround yourselves with people who are in recovery from addiction and are making recovery work for them.

Dialogue 1

<u>January 2001: Pre-Sobriety</u>

A: *Can this be my life? Surely, if there is a God, he made a mistake. Either that or he hates me.*

B: *Why do you say such things?*

A: *Because I'm so $%* confused. My life is just so messed up. If he is so omni-everything, why am I suffering and struggling so much? That's all I'm saying.*

B: *Was it God who made this happen to you or you who made this happen?*

A: *I didn't do this. I don't even want this life I have.*

B: *So you're saying that God is punishing you?*

A: *Apparently . . . no, that's not true either. I don't know what's true anymore. But why is this happening to me; why did this happen to me? God, I swear anything. I will be anything other than a person who is addicted to alcohol. I'll be a nun; I'll do anything—anything but have to give up drinking. I need it. It's like air. I cannot live without it. Even the thought of living without it makes me crave it. Please, please, please . . . I beg you to have mercy on me and take this affliction from me. I just want to be normal, to drink normally. Maybe I just want to sleep; I'll sleep, and everything will be better tomorrow.*

<u>April 2001: Pre-Sobriety</u>

A: *Okay, so today I'm feeling pretty good. I'm sure this will actually be a day of normal drinking. Yep, today I will be a normal drinker. Yes.*

B: *Normal drinkers do not think about drinking normal. They just don't think about drinking at all. It's not an issue for them.*

A: *Shut up; just shut up. I'm trying here.*

June 2001: Pre-Sobriety

A: *Okay, so I drank the whole bottle, but at least I remember the evening. I didn't black out. That's good, right?*

B: *Is this what it has come to? It's okay to drink excessively as long as you don't black out?*

A: *No, that's not what I meant. I meant, I meant . . . I don't know what I meant.*

B: *I know you don't.*

January 2003: Pre-Sobriety

A: *Thank goodness my pregnancy is over. Finally . . . something to calm me.*

B: *Why even get back to drinking?*

A: *Why not? Besides, I just feel better when I drink.*

B: *Really?*

February 2003: Pre-Sobriety

A: *Did I give the kids a bath or did my husband? Did they even get a bath? I'll go see if their towels are still wet. You are a total loser! Don't let him know that you don't know who put the kids to bed last night. Just play it cool and see if he says anything, and then act like you remember. Oh yeah, be nice, be really, really nice—just in case you did something stupid and inappropriate last night. Oh yeah, remember to get the empty bottles into the trash as soon as he leaves the house. Where are they?*

B: *Maybe you could consider not drinking anymore.*

A: *Okay, now that is an obnoxious thought. Do not think that again.*

May 2003: Pre-Sobriety
A: *You need to wrap those bottles in more paper bags before you throw them out. It sounds like a mirror shattering in the garbage truck. God, I hope no one noticed.*

B: *Maybe your drinking is getting a little out of hand?*

A: *Yeah, and maybe not. What do you know, anyway?*

B: *Obviously, I don't know what you know. Is this working for you, Lisa?*

A: *You are such a loser. This cannot be my life.*

August 2003: Pre-Sobriety
A: *You are such a loser. Now the guy who packs your groceries asks why you always buy three bottles of wine. He thinks you have a lot of dinner parties. Ugh, do you think the box boy knows I'm an alcoholic? I'll die if he knows.*

B: *What gives you the idea he doesn't know?*

A: *Well, I am fairly clever.*

B: *Really?*

December 2003: Pre-Sobriety

A: *I do not have an addiction problem, just too much stress. Drinking is fine, smoking pot is fine. As a matter of fact, if I didn't do those things, I'd be horrible to be around. At least I'm bearable.*

B: *Really, do you believe that?*

A: *Yes, most of the time I do . . . truly . . . I do.*

B: *I see it differently.*

A: *Good for you, but you're not the boss.*

B: *Who is the boss? If it's you, do you actually think you're doing a good job with your life?*

A: *Shut up. Just go away and leave me alone.*

B: *We both know that is not possible.*

A: *If I drink more, you'll go away.*

B: *No, you'll just pass out. And when you come to, I will still be here. I'm never going away. I will always be reaching for you.*

A: *I hate that you reach for me.*

B: *That's okay. It doesn't stop me.*

January 2004: Pre-Sobriety
A: *There's no way that just happened. This is just a bad, bad dream, and any second now I will wake up and realize I have been dreaming. Yep, I'm ready to wake up now, any second. NOW, NOW, NOW—THIS IS NOT HAPPENING TO ME. THIS CANNOT BE MY LIFE! How could I let*

this happen to my little daughter? Will she be okay? Just tell me she will be okay. I need a drink!

B: *When are you going to stop, Lisa?*

A: *Tomorrow, I swear. I will stop the drinking tomorrow.*

February 2004: Pre-Sobriety
A: *Help. I need help.*

Part I: The Observation

Observing Our Perspective

Observation is always easy when it is someone else we are observing. We are all good at knowing what others should be doing. We seldom, if ever, scrutinize our own behavior, though. For the most part, we see that we are just fine the way we are, and if any adjusting is needed, it is minor at best. A major overhaul is hardly on our to-do list. News flash: Most unrecovered addicts require a major overhaul. This is not to say that our whole life has to change but that our whole way of *thinking* has to change—my own included. Many of us still have the same spouse, children, house, and car. What we've acquired is a new perspective. Our old perspective kept us drinking; our new perspective keeps us sober.

In my perspective, one of the greatest gifts my dad gave me was the experience of growing up in an unrecovered, alcoholic home. As a child, it was wounding. As an adult, it is the opportunity to cease the lessons and give my children something different—the chance to grow up in a *recovering* alcoholic home. I would never have gotten to this point without my father because, had I not lived through it, I would never have known the lifetime of pain I was about to inflict upon my children.

There are two reasons why we don't stay sober: 1) We don't know how to be a complete person without the aid of an altered consciousness, and 2) we have physically programmed our bodies to function with alcohol.

Both of these issues will need to be addressed if we are to achieve a measure of wholeness and happiness in our lives. If we knew how to function without dependence on alcohol, we would. This is what non-drinkers and "normal" drinkers do. They can function and enjoy life regardless of alcohol consumption. We say we just want to make life more fun. The truth is, we don't know how to have fun or function without our desired drug. It is no longer a choice but a necessity. We just want to think it's a choice, but it's not. We've already programmed our subconscious mind to believe that we need to drink. The subconscious mind isn't so quick to give up this idea.

There are two distinct feelings that every addict is familiar with: 1) a drink must always be there or in our near future so that we can feel right, and 2) being whole without the promise of the former eludes us. We don't know how to be whole—sober and happy. We know how to be *drinking* and happy, but not for a sustained period of time. For most, this "happy" moment lasts twenty seconds to twenty minutes. Then we start thinking about getting more so we can maintain that high. If we can get more, this is good: if we cannot, it is agony. This agony inevitably leads to anxiety, panic, frustration, and unhappiness.

Few of us have experienced wholeness—wholeness in the sense that we are understood and loved for who we are, wholeness in that we could be accepting of life and its infinite challenges. We question that words like *authentic happiness* even belong together. Most of us have never experienced happiness without altering our minds with drugs. Secretly, we crave this moment, and over time we become willing to go to any length to achieve it. Not being whole doesn't bother us, because we believe that if we just continue to get loaded we will be okay. We have conditioned ourselves to seek the drug as the answer, hypnotizing ourselves into thinking that the drug is the way to that wholeness, that completeness we seek.

We have never experienced an unaltered wholeness, and it barely bothers us that we don't know how to achieve this. We have learned that wholeness and happiness elude us because of the lack of one basic component—trust. We don't know how to trust ourselves. We don't have credibility within. We have no navigational tools or guides if we remove the alcohol and drugs.

Alcohol became our guide—our all-encompassing solution to life and its many problems. It made the bad choices seem not so bad and the good choices seem better. Alcohol intensified every feeling we ever had, until one day, all that mattered was the feeling that alcohol created. It was the only feeling we *wanted*. We got to escape into our pretend, private world where everything was just fine—unaddressed, ignored, and chaotic but fine.

Then came the first time that alcohol seemed to turn on us; the honeymoon was over. We were shocked. What had happened to our friend? It wasn't amazing and perfect anymore. What was going on? We asked these questions, and *never* did we like the answer. So we pretended we hadn't heard the answer. We repeatedly tried to make the drugs work, but over time the drugs never worked adequately again. We weren't sure what had happened. All we knew was that the relationship had changed. The infatuation was over, and we felt at fault. We hated that we couldn't make drinking and drugging pure fun anymore. We hunted it down nonetheless. We got into trouble. We finally swore that we would not depend on it any longer.

Then came the seemingly beautiful words we longed to hear. The alcohol said it was *sorry* and that *we should come back*—that *it would be different* this time. We knew secretly that we couldn't live without it. Though we thought we were taking it back, in actuality it was seducing us back. This scenario happened hundreds of times before the fleeting thought came that we had to end this relationship. But we couldn't; we were connected. And nothing, absolutely nothing, could break this bond. *Not* having our alcohol guide was worse than *having* it. We didn't trust it, but we didn't trust ourself either. *It's okay*, said our alcohol guide, and it promised it would be different this time. But it never was; it was worse—slowly worse. We could trust ourself no longer. The noise in our head became harsh and incessant. We no longer trusted others. We did nothing, somehow expecting a miracle. It was enslavement with no escape; we were painfully aware that we were no longer the master.

Through it all, it never occurred to us that happiness is the by-product of a life well lived, not something we experience because we have altered our conscious state. We grant our own happiness. Happiness is a frame of mind. It is not a moment to chase and hang on to, but a moment to be received. We receive happiness because we recognize that happiness is already around us. We don't get the gift of true happiness if we are destroying our life or the lives of those around us. Living life, a fulfilled life, feels nothing like constant indulgence. If we are going for pleasure as a goal to be attained in and of itself, we have missed the target. This is what we did when we drank. We went for the moment of satisfaction—short-term, instant gratification—with no thought for the future. With this new life, we forego the short-term reward for the long-term reward—a reward that lasts a lifetime.

The rewards of a sober life are clearly measurable to those who have achieved them. While addicted, we can only *think* we know how good or not good sobriety might feel, but we never actually know until we experience the rewards. We can want sobriety and imagine the rewards, but until we do the work, we have a limited perspective, a shallow understanding.

If we choose sobriety, we learn what to do to actually achieve it. Sobriety does not happen by chance. We can want it, but if we have no guidelines, tools, or teachers, we will be lost. Finding these resources will be paramount to our success.

How does one begin such a petrifying journey? We make a decision to be open to the idea that something and someone will and can help us. And when that something and someone arrives, we know it, even if it is a fleeting knowledge. It is in that moment of sheer possibility that the seed of sobriety is planted.

This initial incentive for this openness can be something as simple as a conversation, a song, a book, even a commercial. Ideas and opportunities are all around us, and they seem to simply show up. When they do show up and we recognize them, we are tuning in to our potential. We can trust and listen. Many recognize this feeling as inspiration. We know it's there because the feeling resonates deeply within us. It is similar to the pull of a drug, except this connection is healthy.

We all know what that pull feels like. It's the pull we have to the liquor cabinet, the corner store, or that secret place in our closet. It has a voice. It calls. We respond. Until now, that pull may have only been for a drink, but soon the emptiness of that lie will no longer suffice. We again question our relationship with this substance. Somewhere inside us, we need to get this under control, but we don't know how. Still, there will be a beautifully painful wanting, a longing for something; and that something will tell us it's time to move on.

We won't want to move on; we are scared. Yet somehow we hear this same voice again and again. We decide to listen to this person, book, TV show. We aren't even sure we want to be interested. Still, we listen; we're intrigued. What is it that we are hearing? It is time for something to be different in our life. This is our way out. We see that we might not be alone after all. Someone else has felt what we feel and can help us.

That someone will show us through action (not just words) what it means to be trustworthy. He or she will show us that trust is the path to long-term sobriety. We are not speaking of a blind or foolish trust. We are talking of a surprising resonance with another person whom our heart has welcomed. Through that person, we will begin to experience what it feels like to trust again. As we watch that person walk through life unaltered, we will see that it is possible for us too.

Use this book as one resource. That is its purpose. We do not heal alone. It is highly unlikely that we will accomplish such a feat without the proper guidance. It is too big.

We begin by identifying who we want to be in our life *today*, not somewhere down the line when we have a few days or months strung together but today, now—*right now*.

Most of us, however, can only relate to yesterday's behavior. It is difficult to believe we can be anything different from what we have always been. For many, it's impossible. That's why we stay in a holding pattern—the perpetual orbit of unending misery. Getting our head into today is the most important step in living in the present. More aptly, getting our head into this moment is the first step in living in this moment. If our trying-to-get-sober experience has been tumultuous, there is no need to fret. This work is doable. Recovery does have a life of its own and doesn't have to include relapse. If we have relapsed, we don't need to have another one, ever.

Dialogue 2

<u>March 2004: Sobriety—Day 2</u>

A: *Can this be my life? The world hates me.*

B: *Detox is the safest place for you to be. You tried to quit on your own, but you couldn't do it. Get over it.*

A: *Look at these people. This is what my life has come to? Ugh. I'll stop drinking for one year, just one year. I'll get things under control for a while and learn how to drink normally. After all, what if I'm not an alcoholic? Yes, any normal drinker could easily go a year without drinking!*

B: *Maybe you could try to focus on today instead of a year from now?*

A: *Why should I?*

B: *Because a year is a long time away.*

A: *Good, then it's decided . . . one year, no drinking.*

B: *Are you listening?*

A: *Not really. I've already made my decision. I've got this under control. Trust me.*

Observing Our Words

This is as important as anything else we will understand in this book, maybe even the most important: *to learn what words actually mean to us*. We begin to recognize how much comes out of our mouth that is thoughtless, talking for the sake of talking. We will see how little energy goes into the words we choose and the way we deliver them. We will learn to stop saying words we don't intend and to start searching for the words that accurately express the idea we do intend. We will have a greater understanding of our intention when we slow down our mouth. We will be clearer about our motive when we think before we speak. Our ability to communicate coherently will be the result of our awareness of self—what's truthfully going on, not what we want to pretend is going on.

While initially we may think our words are accurate, closer investigation will show that we lack integrity. We'll say what we should, what we think others want to hear. We'll say whatever flies out first, even if we have no intention of following through with it. Sometimes we say "white lies" because they have a speck of truth, and that's enough for us. What we will learn to say is the truth—the truth as it applies to us. And this can look vastly different from what we are used to saying. Sometimes the truth is: we don't know; we'll have an answer later; we're scared to say the truth; or we're not interested in the truth. While none of these will be what the other person wants to hear, they are accurate. They are not a lie. We are beginning to learn how not to lie.

The phrase "Say what you mean, and mean what you say" is familiar to most of us—so familiar that we take it for granted. Don't say that we *can* when we *can't* or that we *will* when we *won't*. It's simple. Begin to notice how seldom the truthful words appear because we have conditioned ourselves to lie instead. We all have a conscience that knows if we are lying or not. Use it. Sometimes when we first try this, it is difficult because we are so used to not telling the truth. It's okay if we mess up; we just keep trying. We will notice, over time, that it gets easier, and the outcome is far less complicated to handle. The reason we lie is because we feel we have something we need to protect. If we allow the truth to be seen, we are

25

risking a loss. We don't want to risk losing whatever it is we are protecting, so we lie. Observing and identifying what we are afraid of losing will take some digging and questioning on our part.

If we are new to sobriety or have struggled to maintain it, we may have confused *choosing* to stop drinking with wanting to *want* to stop. These are vastly different starting points. The first means that we are done drinking. The second leaves a back door, an escape hatch.

Choosing to stop drinking indicates that we can identify with the desire to be done drinking. We have made a decision that alcohol and drugs are no longer working for us. While we may not be clear on what this entails, anything is better than what we currently have. While we are scared, the fear of moving forward does not seem as horrible as the fear of staying where we are. On a fear scale of one to ten, staying where we are is a ten. Moving forward and figuring out sobriety ranks around a nine and a half.

Wanting to want to stop drinking indicates that we can see some of the benefits of stopping drinking, but we rationalize our situation, and thus the decision goes unmade. We would like to want to, but for now we can easily convince ourselves that it is not the best choice. We can still see the perceived benefits of drinking, and for the present, the benefits still outweigh the consequences.

Knowing where we stand will determine the starting point. If we don't want sobriety, we shouldn't pretend to want it when what we really want is to drink without the undesirable consequences. Nothing short of more "experiences" will determine the final outcome. By "experiences" we mean more damaging repercussions. It's redundant, but true: We're done when we're done and not a moment sooner. We can't fake it or psych ourselves into believing something other than what we believe. Willing ourselves to believe something we don't believe has never worked.

Here is an example how the process (change) might appear when shifting from one belief to that belief's opposite:

1. I am definitely not an alcoholic.
2. I might be an over-drinker at times.
3. I might have some alcoholic tendencies, but I could get them under control if I wanted to. I just don't want to.

4. I don't always drink alcoholically, but sometimes I do.
5. It seems like it might be a problem, but a small one.
6. It is definitely a problem, but I could turn it around if there wasn't so much stress.
7. It's definitely a problem, and I can't seem to stop even when I try.
8. I am definitely an alcoholic.

If we are wondering if sobriety is the path for us, we are encouraged take an honest look at where we now stand. This process can take months, years, or decades. It's our story, and we get to decide.

Observing and Awareness

We can stop saying we want something that we don't really want. We're lying to ourselves, and it is killing us. Admitting that we don't know something leaves room for us to learn a new idea and make an educated decision before the decision gets made for us. If we think we already know everything, what is there to learn or explore? Nothing! That place of nothing is immobilizing us. We are stuck thinking that we already have all the answers when, in actuality, we have *no* answers.

Finding our identity means that we are always learning, creating, and growing. Identity isn't stagnant. It is always moving forward into a newer version of something more. Even our addiction is not stagnant. It is always growing into something more. Unfortunately, that something more isn't making our life any better. In fact, it is making us more unhappy, more confused, more alone, more dependent, less free. The trade-off seems so simple, so impossibly simple! Yet we still look for another way—until we do not.

Most times the seemingly small shifts we make in our thinking yield the greatest outcome—for example, when *I can't* is truthfully *I don't want to*. The words *I can't* imply that it is impossible, while the words *I don't want to* mean exactly that. They mean that we could if we wanted to; we just don't want to—regardless of the implications. These are extremely different points of view. We begin to change when we have the awareness that we haven't been willing, wanting, or open to change. We would save time by being honest. Why don't we want to? Because we think we already have all the answers. What are we trying to protect? An identity that no longer serves us. What are we working so hard to preserve? Our perception of freedom and our right to drink.

When we begin to question our awareness of our own feelings, we are equally perplexed. A question like *How are you feeling?* can send us reeling. For most, the answer falls into a general category: good, bad, or fine. Good might mean elated, pleased, content, or adequate. Bad might mean devastated, blue, awkward, depressed, or sick. Fine might mean furious, disappointed, pissed-off, bored, or lonely.

Learning to decipher exactly what we are feeling will be a huge leap toward a stable identity. We will no longer be meeting our needs with that all-inclusive pseudo-solution of alcohol and drugs. We will be identifying and solving problems at a new level. We will begin to distinguish what a feeling actually is and which one we are having. When we are aware of our feelings, we are more capable of getting our goals met.

Words are powerful. Nothing, however, is more powerful than the way we act. Our actions speak louder than our words 100 percent of the time. How we behave is the clearest indicator of what we believe to be true for us. We can't fake ourselves out—at least not for long. The truth is relentless. It will eventually catch up with us. We all get to a point where our denial of something simply makes no sense anymore. Everyone has a breaking point. There are only so many excuses we can hide behind. Eventually these will dry up. One by one, they will no longer work. Then we will be granted the ability to see the holes in our armor. Our story stopped sounding authentic to many others long ago. It is finally reaching us.

With this thought, we begin the process we call recovery. We recover from a state of mind that has held us hostage within our own body and mind. Bruce Lipton, cellular biologist and author, states, "Our success is based on our choices, which are, in turn, totally dependent on our awareness."[1]

First Challenge: Start observing your behavior. Become aware of something new about yourself daily.

Dialogue 3

A: *Well, I've eliminated the alcohol, but I'm as messed up as ever. How did I get so screwed up?*

B: *You can do this. Just stay focused on today.*

A: *Remember, it's for a year. I can't make it a year. I hate sobriety. Life is so painful. I hate this. I hate you, and I hate me. How am I going to do this? I can't do this sober thing.*

B: *Just for today. You're not drinking just for today.*

A: *Okay, I can do that—just today. Maybe tomorrow. Tomorrow is Friday. That will be a good day to start drinking again. But not today. Okay.*

B: *Okay.*

Part II: The Process

Learning to Create a Plan

All change has a progression. Change *is* progression, a natural course that occurs for the end result to appear. Even without our conscious thought, a process can occur. If we are thirsty, first we get the thought, *I am thirsty*; and from there we get a glass and fill it with water. No one thinks about this process. It just happens naturally; unless, of course, we are desolate in the Sahara where getting water is an issue. What probably goes unnoticed as a process in our kitchen becomes a survival mission in the desert. When necessity is the driving force, we must engage the conscious mind for assistance. Process is always happening, and the necessity to engage consciously is determined by our familiarity with the environment. If we have a reference point or familiarity from a previous situation, the subconscious easily overrides the need for conscious thought.

If we feel that we want something other than what we currently have, we are required to do a lot more conscious thinking. We will want a rough draft of how we are going to begin the process of achieving something new. Leaving it to chance is the equivalent of leaving it alone. Just because we have a vision doesn't mean we have a plan. A vision is a starting point, a place where we feel we have the desire for something—a spark, an idea, an inspiration. A plan consists of the actual steps we are going to take to get us where we want to go.

Both vision and a plan are necessary to reach our goal. Until now, we have thought we could proceed in recovery without a plan. This has inevitably left us with little or no chance of success. Maybe we've even

31

had a partial plan, but results were slow, and we eventually abandoned the idea. If we are to succeed, we will want to design an achievable plan.

Have we ever had a plan to guide us through sobriety? For most of us the answer is *no*. Today we are going to begin the process of acquiring a workable plan. Let's look at a simple example first. The desire: Get some ice cream. Plan A: 1) Get wallet, 2) drive to store, 3) purchase ice cream, 4) drive home, 5) take out of bag, and 6) eat.

For argument's sake, let's say our ice cream shop is closed. What do we do then? Plan B: 1) get angry or not, 2) decide if ice cream is imperative, 3) if it is, decide where else we can go, 4) decide if it is worth the drive, and 5) if it is, complete steps two through six in Plan A. This small interruption has created four new steps in the middle of our original plan.

This is an elementary example of a plan. Nonetheless, it shows the process. What about something as complex as acquiring a sober identity? Sobriety is not a simple, six-step task and will require more than one plan, as well as numerous modifications. When the situation is familiar, planning is easy; when the situation is unfamiliar, planning requires effort. The work ahead is the beginning framework upon which we will design our plan.

Sometimes we start making our plans before we're even aware of our desire. We just want something, anything. It's like going to the grocery store when we're hungry. It yields mostly impulse foods: pre-packaged, quick-fix satisfaction, all because of a frenzied, hungry state of mind.

The first step is to quiet our mind. This can include journaling, jogging, listening to calming music, or taking a relaxing walk. Whatever we choose, it should be something that brings peacefulness rather than revving us up. From there, we can make our list of intentions. Whatever they are, write them down. Note that some goals can be completed quickly, while others require that we be content to watch them grow slowly. Whatever we write, whatever we want, we must make sure it is our truth. There's no point in writing down lies or what we think others would want us to write. That won't work! The goal here is to really want what's on your list and be willing to work toward it. This is not to say that the list and the goals won't change—they will. It is to show the starting point for what we believe we desire today, so our tomorrows can be more of what we designed.

Choose words with thoughtful intention. Know what it is you want. Search for the exact words. There are times when we act as if we do not care about an outcome when indeed we do. We pretend to be okay, because we are used to letting ourselves down in the past. Do not be afraid to revisit these desires. If they are ever to come to fruition, they will need to be brought to honest awareness. Partial awareness is equivalent to no awareness. We either choose something or we do not. Be honest. Even if we do not know, we can be honest about the fact that we don't know. Our genuine desire or intention produces the discovery of our truth; it always does. Always.

Sometimes we say we don't want something because we are afraid of the magnitude of work involved in achieving the desired outcome. We must try not to let this hinder our new identity. While we realize it may hinder our vision, recognize that this setback is illusory. It can and will pass quickly if we let it. Our achievement of anything is in seeing that we have the ability to overcome our perceived fears. For now, we simply begin to trust the process. We're allowed to design our life. In fact, we are the only one who can.

So when we hear that voice inside telling us how foolish it is to dream that life could be different, we must not listen to it. This voice is not our higher self trying to move us forward but our lower self trying to hold us back. It will continue to speak. We decide if we will listen. The voice that prevails is the one we listen to and feed.

Second Challenge: Discover whether or not you actually want what it is you say you want. Are your actions in alignment with your desire? If not, what kind of changes are you prepared to make? Journal as much detail as possible. Remember, do not cut corners, and above all else, do not give in to hopelessness. Have faith that this process can work for you.

It's Not Hopeless

One moment we think we have hope; the next we are hopeless. It can be difficult to identify the shift because it happens quickly. Hope is the longing for something we don't currently have. Hopelessness means wanting something but giving up on ever having it. We've quit trying. Hope and hopelessness are both temporary and momentary frames of mind. One second we want something, and the next we don't. We needn't worry. This is normal. The good news is that even a small dose of hope can put us in a position for something different to happen. Hope makes the difference between probable and possible. Being willing to see that our desire is possible for us will be a necessary step toward recovery. Otherwise, our choices are too limited.

Our subconscious mind is powerful and can lock us into a way of thinking that will handicap us in the long run. Note: It is not required that we have action steps or even a plan at this juncture. A simple wanting is all that is required. A defeated attitude will only prolong our unwarranted frame of mind. Our belief that we don't deserve anything better will actually produce more of what we don't want. As soon as we recognize that we are doing this, we must *stop* and observe our thinking. Most situations are not hopeless, not even ours. We just don't know how to receive the answer to the problem—yet.

Do we have faith? Do we believe this achievement is possible for us? The word *faith* tells us that we have no visible proof. It means we cannot prove the outcome. Belief is a knowing, an intuition that is based on evidence. We see it as a possibility, a seed of potential. Placed in the proper environment, belief will flourish. Left in the wrong environment, it will die.

The idea behind faith is that we needn't have a plan outlined. We only need a knowing. This knowing will allow the necessary resources to present themselves into our life. For example, we decide we want to run a marathon. We have never run before, but we have faith that we can learn. Resources appear that support us—a trainer, a book on running, or a new friend who loves to run. From faith, we move toward a place of belief.

We believe because we have a measure of proof that it is possible. Again, we want to run a marathon, and because we've previously run a 10k, we believe that with the proper planning and training we can accomplish it. Our belief comes from our past experience. With this level of thinking, it is not only possible but probable that we can and will train, if that is our desire.

We see ourselves as hopeless when we feel devastated. We experience no movement, and in many instances, we don't even care. We've abandoned hope.

We are hopeful when we recognize that the future holds promise for us. When there is promise, we have something to hold onto, a reason to continue moving forward. Faith is something that is possible. If faith is acknowledged and placed in the proper environment, it will flourish. Belief produces potential and probability because of our past experience.

It's not a coincidence that people who believe they can accomplish something do. Getting ourself to this position is a chief aim of this book. We begin by having faith that we can trust ourselves again. We give ourselves permission to believe that change is possible, because it *is* possible. Taking action on these steps *proves* to us that something is possible. Acting on our trusted voice rather than on our frantic, urgent voice will produce achievement.

This isn't just a theory; this is a fact. The questions to ask ourselves are: 1) Do we really want this, and 2) Are we willing to work toward achieving it? These aren't essay questions. They are *yes* or *no* questions. Many times, the answer is no, but we say yes anyway. Why do we do this? We do it to get people to leave us alone.

When our chief aim is clear, the path may change, but the destination remains the destination. In this case, the destination is continued sobriety. We always know what our chief aim is because it is revealed by what we currently possess. If getting alcohol is on our list of must-do tasks today, it is safe to say that we are not interested in getting sober. People who want to get sober are looking for a way to *avoid* obtaining alcohol. They are taking action that is contrary to acquiring alcohol. If our chief aim is to go to bed sober tonight, we do whatever it takes to make that happen.

From the onset, we focus on the end result in order to reach it. Exactly what we do does not matter. What matters is that we do whatever it takes. What matters is that we discover what we want. Only we can answer that question. It's a life's work done a moment at a time. Once we realize that we can face fears and beliefs that once would have killed us, we are gaining wisdom. Once we walk safely through the temptation, we save the template. If we've done it once, we can do it again.

We do not give in to hopelessness; instead we have hope. If we have faith in the process, we will come to trust and believe strongly in it.

Learned Beliefs

Learned beliefs are those things we have believed all our lives to be true. If everyone tells us that something is true, we adopt an attitude and lifestyle based on the belief that it is true. If it is a positive belief, it is safe to say that it does not have an adverse effect on us. Example: *I'm really good at my job.* If it's a negative belief (*I'll never amount to much*), it is safe to say it is holding us back. In many cases, we may not have thought much about whether or not something is true; we have simply taken it at face value because someone said it was so. If someone said it often enough, we accepted it as true. We subconsciously adopted it as a belief.

Such beliefs are limiting because they prevent us from seeing their falseness. They hold us hostage in our lives. We believe them to be true. And because we believe them to be true, we ignore anything that doesn't align with them. We consequently walk away from opportunities that could be life-altering—for the better. The problem is that we aren't even aware that we have walked away from something. Nor are we aware that we even have these limiting thoughts. Only through deep, subconscious work will we begin to uncover them.

We will be working on identifying and eliminating these limiting beliefs. Eliminating beliefs means we see the non-truth of them. We see their falseness, that they are not functional. Achieving sobriety means we will spend our lives becoming aware and growing through these beliefs.

This is not so much a recovery tool, but rather a life tool. No person is exempt from growth. We don't address these beliefs all at once. Rather, we focus on what is most pressing—that situation or discomfort that is staring us square in the eyes, the current condition of our life. We grow continuously as situations present themselves to us. If we are to live life fully, we need to engage in life fully. It requires effort to see these beliefs. Denying that we have limiting beliefs causes the problem. As we deal with our fears and face them, we find that they don't have the power we once thought. It is when we don't inquire, when we ignore and deny, that we face the hardest struggle.

Our subconscious mind is programmed not to entertain new information that will challenge us. Therefore, it keeps its distance from new experiences. Supposedly, our limiting beliefs keep us safe—safe from challenges, discomfort, rejection, and change. Unfortunately, these opportunities generally show up as problems, sticky issues, confrontations, or burdens. The mind is quick to reject these new ideas. It needs to reject them, because not to reject them means admitting that there is error in our thinking. No one wants to think that he is thinking wrong. Because the subconscious mind is quick to reject, it must then criticize in order to feel good about not learning, participating, or taking on a challenge. This in turn reinforces the familiar, limiting belief system, and we stay stuck, believing that everything we believe is the truth.

We hold beliefs both consciously and subconsciously. The beliefs we will be questioning are stored in our subconscious mind and are programmed at a cellular level. We only learn that we have them because of the path our life has taken. We see evidence of these beliefs in the current conditions of our lives; our health, finances, and lifestyle are by-products of our personal belief system.

Identifying where we are stuck will require awareness at a conscious level. Once we actually observe our thinking and behavior, we are able to change it. We consciously recognize our mental blocks and begin the work of reprogramming them at a subconscious level. Recognition is pivotal to change.

Third Challenge: Make a list of limiting beliefs that you are aware you have. If you are drawing a blank, these tag words may help: a negative mantra you repeat; prejudices for people, places, or institutions; strong opinions regarding sex, money, education, government, or religion. Add to this list as awareness increases. Once you have identified a belief, notice how that belief affects your behavior. Next, identify what could happen if you stopped behaving according to those thoughts. Journal your answers.

Want or Need

The average person, over time, has a tendency to stop pursuing new goals. We believe that dreaming, creativity, and inspiration are for the young, forgetting that we always have life ahead of us. We feel that if we were going to arrive, we should have done so already. At some point, there is a stage in our lives where we accept the situation, believing that no matter where we are, this is as good as it gets. Very little time is spent cultivating new skill sets, tools, or data. If we are to achieve lasting sobriety, we need to be willing to learn and apply new information. We can't want something new and then expect it to just appear. That is not going to happen.

If we do decide we want to learn something new, a *vehicle* will show up to get us moving in that direction. The end result doesn't simply appear. What appears is a tool to help us achieve the end result. For addicts, this is not great news. We want it, and we want it now. We have little tolerance for waiting. We typically want to put the minimum amount of effort into acquiring something new, and we certainly don't want to have to be uncomfortable, at least not for long. We have spent most of our time going for what's easy and comfortable, for what we think we want rather than what we actually need. Our efforts have been half-hearted at best and completely shallow and self-seeking at worst.

Unless we can sustain some discomfort, we are destined for a life of unhealthy dependency. Not just dependency on drugs. All manner of addiction falls into this category. Addiction is the unhealthy need to rely on something outside of us to make us feel right on the inside. We imagine we will be free if we can just have the drink, but it never produces the freedom we want. More often than not, it produces unwanted outcomes.

There are two paths that lie in front of us. Path One is familiar. It is more of the same, getting high for a few moments of delusional freedom. Path Two is unfamiliar. It involves deciding to do things differently. This requires actual time spent consciously working on yourself. When we work on ourself from the inside out, we acquire a lifetime of freedom. Seems like an easy choice, doesn't it?

But it's not for an addict. The problem is that we are petrified. We're scared of who is living inside us without our alcohol and drugs. Who would we be? We feel our body would explode into a million pieces if we didn't get our fix. It's this belief (limiting as it is) that is real for us. We believe it, and so it is! It will continue to be this way until we acquire a measure of trust. Until we make the shift at a subconscious level, we will hold steadfast to this perceived belief. We don't know how to live in the real world. We never look at what we have the opportunity to do, to be, or to say—so that we can start to achieve our dreams.

Let's assume we are feeling stuck in our sobriety. Maybe a little bored or overly frustrated. Whatever it is, there is a way to see and solve it, but only if we choose. The answer will arrive. It might not be the answer we prefer, but nonetheless, it's the answer. We know it's the answer because it's what has shown up. Here is what often happens. The answer arrives, and we don't like it, so somehow we think this is an excuse to not do anything except complain and blame. The answer is the answer! Just because we don't like it has nothing to do with it. We had a question. We got an answer—one we didn't like—and somehow we decided that we never got an answer or that the answer we got was wrong.

Can we give the answer a try? No, we don't want to, because then we might be out of our comfort zone. We don't want that; we can't bear that. Even the thought of being in discomfort makes us want to drink. And still, the answer remains the answer. We want the universe to give us a green light to behave any way we choose, with no repercussions for our actions. The universe simply does not work this way. The imbalance would be too great. So the universe gives us what we *need* to keep life balanced, not what we *want* so we can go on destroying.

The goal is to see the point at which we consistently give up on achieving our sobriety. It is generally the same threshold. When we get there, we quit every time. Where have we cut our vision short because we were not willing to endure some discomfort? Was it the drive past the liquor store, judgment of a twelve-step program, or contempt for a therapist? Was the solution as simple as making a phone call to a trusted friend and asking for help? Whatever the conditions were, we will repeat the scenario until we become aware of where we consistently quit when we selfishly choose what we *want* instead of what we *need*.

Fourth Challenge: Start to notice when you get what you need rather than what (you think) you want. Recognize the gift that arrived at this moment. Feel and express gratitude that it happened the way it did. Journal your findings.

Sickly Familiar

We all know how it feels when it's really hot and we walk into an air-conditioned room. It's an *ahhhh* feeling. We love the cool. We love it because we've been extremely hot. If we had just been in a snowstorm, it wouldn't feel so great. Instead we'd be looking for a heater to warm us. So which one feels best? It depends on where we've been. The familiar always feels familiar. We're accustomed to it. We only notice when it gets extreme.

For addicts, this is an all-too-common pendulum swing. We experience the extremes of either drinking too much or being bored by sobriety (or *slow-briety*, as it is sometimes called). We can handle the extreme, or at least we think we can. We just promise everyone that we'll get sober, whether we mean it or not. The feeling of boredom, however, is torture for an unrecovered addict. When the chaos of our external world is quiet, we are left with the chaos in our heads. This we cannot stand. We don't want to feel the dullness of life unaltered by alcohol. We are used to—and thrive on—the chaos that accompanies drinking. If we are newly sober, these calm moments can be threatening, and they can quickly be eliminated with a drink, which is a poor choice if we are going for recovery.

What do we do with this feeling? For now, it simply needs to be acknowledged for what it is—a feeling. It is not a fact, just a feeling; and feelings pass. When we remember that we seek the familiar, it is no mystery why we are so uncomfortable when we are newly sober. Everything we have been shoving down with drugs is now at its boiling point. And it will continue to boil until we turn down the heat in our heads, which we do by getting honest about the truth of our addiction and who we have become.

Just because it is familiar in no way means it is acceptable. We are sadly addicted to a life that is well below our own standards. We have settled. We've lowered our criteria so that we could feel comfortable with our sick life.

Fifth Challenge: Notice and list standards that are currently in place in your life. Which of these standards is beneath the person you thought you would become? Why has it become acceptable to live this way? Journal about each standard.

A Motivated Process

Why is it so important to a have a process, a plan? The Plan—the steps we take to achieve something—when used properly, can drive and move us in ways and directions that nothing else can. It's the difference between crawling and walking. Both will get us there, but one will get us there faster and with less pain. The Plan comes from the core of us; it is created, designed, honed, and implemented 100 percent by us. There is no chance for failure, because we set the agenda as well as the pace. It's foolproof when used with the proper mind-set. And what's the proper mind-set? One of possibility, probability, work, and commitment.

Do we know what motivates us? Many of us do not. We know that we like to get loaded, but beyond that we aren't certain. We aren't sure what or how the voice of motivation and encouragement might sound. We thought we knew the voice of motivation when we wanted a fix, but that's not motivation. That's craving. That's addiction. Learning how to get motivated and stay encouraged is required learning.

A motive is a need or desire that causes a person to act. Our motives can be instigated by our desire for comfort, recognition, rewards, fear, satisfaction, revenge, love, punishment, stability, security, fame, money, necessities (food and shelter), and/or connection. If we are honest, most of us can admit that we have been motivated by each of these desires. The patterns we developed earliest are the patterns that we repeat.

When faced with a familiar situation, we are generally motivated to behave the way we have always behaved. Author Bruce Lipton states, "The most powerful and influential programs in the subconscious mind are the ones that were recorded first."[1] We've developed patterns that make us susceptible to being swayed by someone else's agenda as well as patterns that cause us to dig in our heels and be headstrong. It all depends on what's at stake and who we perceive to be in charge.

Most of us enjoy recognition. When we don't get it—even when we are 100 percent committed—we have trouble staying motivated. The key is to give ourselves these much-needed accolades. As we learn how to recognize our own efforts, we can move forward, energized and excited despite the challenges that lie ahead.

The key is to check our motivation. Once we determine that it is clean, we can give ourselves what we need to move ahead. If we don't know what we need to stay motivated, we can't supply it. If we are only motivated from a place of fear and consequences, we will stay paralyzed and stuck. If the need or desire to succeed isn't 100 percent ours, the required energy will never manifest. And if by chance we do achieve that need or desire, we find that one of two things has happened: 1) we secretly did want it (even a little), or 2) we now have something we resent having, and it's meaningless to us.

Regardless of which one is true, there is knowledge to be gained. If it is the former, we get to see that we really did want the achievement. If it is the latter, we get to see that we have abandoned ourself and then begin cultivating a stronger bond with our higher self, the self that knows how to be true to us and take care of us. Either way, we will be changing, but only if we are willing to observe our thinking as well as our actions.

Motives can be tricky at first, especially if we have grown accustomed to manipulating ourself and others. As we work at checking our motives, we will acquire a skill for identifying where we are going. When the goal is clear, we will be willing to work through the obstacles that present themselves.

If we are venturing to a mountain's peak, we must, with certainty and intent, want to reach the top. If we aren't clear at the onset, at our point-of-origin, the challenge of the climb will not be worth our effort. It's that simple. We will quit. We might not quit right away in that moment or that week or even that month, but eventually we will quit.

Not only will we quit, we'll provide an overly detailed list of reasons why we had to quit and how it was for the best. We will want others to support our quitting. If they do not, we will perceive them as being wrong. Our lies, our stories have become our identity. And all of this mess is created because we lack the ability to be honest about who we are and what we want. We do not trust ourselves and our ability to achieve. The longer this mode lasts, the more ingrained it becomes in our minds. It is sickly normal. It is insane, and we cannot see it.

We move away from insanity by consciously thinking soundly. We read the words on the page and see how they apply to us rather than pretend they are not for us. If a craving is our only starting point for motivation, we have a lot of work to do. If we are constantly craving, we have set our sights on very little in this life. We are living in a fantasy. We have not given the seed of potential even a glance, let alone soil, sun, and water.

Finding our motivation is our next big step. Below are motivational guidelines to help us identify who we are and who we intend to become. Motives are best when:

1. They make us feel good about ourselves.
2. They come from love.

3. We have no hidden scheme.
4. We are not doing something solely to make someone else happy at the risk of harming ourselves.

The sum of the above qualities is *integrity.* Our integrity is our actual starting point in the Plan.

Here's an example. If we want to go to Hawaii for vacation, we will want a flight going into Honolulu. We know our destination, but what is our point of origin? Are we booking out of Los Angeles or New York City? We must know our starting point. We have our ticket, a Honolulu map, a brochure, bags packed, and a flight that's leaving at noon. But if we're in New York City and should be in Los Angeles, we've missed our plane. Nothing else will matter if we haven't identified our origin.

How do we define our *origin,* our Point O? We begin by learning about our mind and how it works. For now, let's understand that our Point O is as important as our destination—our Point D.

Sixth Challenge: Learn what motivates you. Begin identifying patterns that are repetitive. If you are struggling, look back at early childhood achievements and work forward. See if a pattern appears. Journal about achievements that came to fruition as well as those that did not. Both will be revealing.

Sustained Motivation

Motivation is sustained through continued awareness of what has been achieved, no matter how insignificant it may seem, including extended effort to set new goals. Stephen Covey, author of *The 7 Habits of Highly Effective People,* suggests that we set a new goal prior to the completion of the current goal. In this way, we direct our energy toward something new rather than sit and rest on past achievements. It is important that we recognize small markers of achievement as well as set up new targets to achieve. We keep our motivation sustained because we have identified targets that we really want. No one is motivated all the time. We all require moments to rejuvenate our mind and body. Enjoy these when they arrive rather than feeling guilty about downtime. Do something enjoyable. Remembering, the car gets refueled if it is to run.

Suffice it to say, my early sobriety was often filled with a nagging incompleteness. I was driven to set goals and achieve, but still something was awry. Sobriety was definitely better than drinking, but it was still not fulfilling enough. I wanted more out of life than to be sober. I wanted to be filled, but I wasn't sure with what. I could not identify the source of my emptiness, but I was determined to find my Point O. Additionally, I was and am a member of a twelve-step program. To the best of my ability, I had completed my step work as outlined. I had expected my life to feel better, a *lot* better. I felt clear that drinking was not the answer, but I must admit there were many moments when drinking passed through my mind. After all, that had been the tool I used for most of my adult life. I recognized it as that "sickly familiar" feeling and managed to grab some other tools. Again, I reached out for help.

I was introduced to my first *life coach*. A life coach is a person who helps you navigate your life. In many ways, they are similar to a coach for a sports team. A good coach digs at you emotionally with thought provoking and relevant questions. They challenge you to get clarity. They help you move through obstacles. They push you toward a peak performance. They challenge your ideas and beliefs about life. They encourage and motivate. As my life coach and I sat together talking, I got a glimpse that this relationship might move me forward.

We discussed life and what I was willing to do to move forward. I put my pen to paper, or rather fingers to keyboard, and started some inquiry with myself. What did I really want? I wasn't going to drink (at least not today). There had to be more to life than just staying sober. I began to look back at all the dreams I had dismissed along the way. No matter how far-fetched they seemed, I wrote them down—all of them! The next step was to see which ones were short-term and doable. After that, I could move on to the long-term and doable. These were my first attempts at creating a plan for what would be my life. It is nothing short of extraordinary when I look back to that day.

I finally had something new to focus on, something other than not drinking. This "thing" was called *my life*. What did I want for my life? I became focused on what I wanted to become in this lifetime: a friend, cook, mom, athlete, life coach, author, and pianist. Anything I could dream up went on the list. I started with the small things—like making the family a nice dinner every night and folding the laundry with gratitude for a washer and dryer. I focused on learning how to love my kids for who they were and not for who I wanted them to be. I began to see them as individuals with their own journeys. I began to meditate, exercise, pray, and care for my body. Do you know what began to happen? I became a friend worth having, a wonderful cook, a bona fide mom, a runner, and a triathlete. I went back to school and became a life coach and a recovery coach. I'm still working on becoming the pianist.

My life was changing. I felt I made great progress in a short period of time—all because I was willing to identify desires, document a possible plan, and discipline myself to stick with the plan. It just seemed too simple, and it *was* simple. The key for me was accountability. At first, I was driven by accountability to my coach. As time passed, however, I grew to appreciate accountability to myself. I had been empty inside because my word had been no good to me. Now I was learning to be true to myself as well as to those around me.

It all started within me. My inside felt clean—a feeling I had never known. And while I lovingly welcomed the relief, I felt sadness for those who struggled around me. I wanted to help them but did not see how. I came to realize that if I was ever to help another, I would have to learn with and through myself first. Over time, I began to see the world from a radically different perspective—a world in which I was the co-creator of my destiny. The universe wasn't working against me but with and for me. My lack of understanding of the universal laws, the basic principles of life, was what was holding me back from understanding myself.

This became a journey of understanding me—today. Not the old me I had been in the past, but the person who was here right now. I began by observing my thinking and my behavior—today. This was my starting point (Point O, point-of-origin). How I behaved *today* was the real me. I could no longer pretend. It was both insightful and horrifying, yet it filled that emptiness within. Who would have thought that accepting my inner truth about who I really was could be the answer to freedom? Certainly not this alcoholic girl. Once I saw the truth, I could go anywhere from there. I set out to find a new me—an identity that resonated deeply.

Here was and still is my identity criteria: a pureness of motive (despite my more-than-tainted history); a willingness to become the best possible version of myself (the best I am capable of that day); a determined desire to grow (whichever direction is best); and an attitude of forgiveness (genuine, not feigned forgiveness).

This is the model (Appendix A) I designed, which is my model for living. I refer to it as the 4D Design:

1. **Desire:** My deepest want.
2. **Decision:** I have made a clear choice to pursue this.
3. **Dedication:** I will stay committed, regardless of obstacles.
4. **Destination:** I will arrive.

This is not a model I had previously used. The model for most of my life looked more like my model for lying to myself. I refer to that as the Self-WILL Design.

1. **Whimsical wants:** I want it all, and I want it when I want it.
2. **Indecision:** I just can't make up my mind.
3. **Lazy:** I'll be dedicated, but only until it gets hard. Then I'll quit.
4. **Lost:** I'll never arrive.

This model never worked, despite my many attempts. If I was to achieve something new, it was clear that I needed to put forth some new energy. I was tired of being in pain, so I stopped drinking. Now, I'd become tired of engaging in the (almost constant) battle in my head. Life was on, and I was excited again—or maybe even for the first time—to live. I was learning how to think. This would be the catalyst to my metamorphosis. The tools were there. I just hadn't known how to see them. But I was determined to learn.

When we willingly work with another (i.e., a life coach, therapist, counselor, twelve-step sponsor), we no longer walk through the process alone. This is key to recovery that lasts. Our thinking is no longer the main—and in some cases, sole—source of information. Not only will these partners introduce new ideas, they will cause us to question our views. They awaken us to possibilities, ones that have never entered our minds. They introduce us to like-minded people through recovery groups, twelve-step meetings, social outings, seminars, and conferences. They share how they have recovered, and they help us find our path.

I am now in a position to offer to another what has been offered to me. As a life-skills and recovery coach, I work with recovering addicts. We begin the process of transitioning from the sell-WILL Design to the 4D Design. The client shares his or her newfound desire. I help him or her through listening, asking questions for clarification, and pointing out inconsistencies or polarities in their desire. Once the desire is clear and has merit, they move toward making a decision to achieve it. I support them through listening and clarifying that decision. Next, they create a written action plan, and I suggest some challenges. The action plan allows them to see the next step as well as the progress they have made. The challenges allow them to see their sense of conviction.

When they are in the stage of dedication, I offer encouragement, support, facts, inspiration, new data, reminders, and measures of success. These are all attributes that can be difficult to call forth from self, for self. It is much easier to support others when my own agenda is not attached. My only agenda is to support my client in achieving what he says he wants. I am here to hold him accountable. The client's mind will talk him out of this accountability, but *my* mind will not.

Finding a coach can make all the difference in the quality of our sobriety. I personally believe that having a life coach was the next best step I took in my sobriety. I set a strong foundation with a twelve-step program and continued to grow from that time forward.

Here are some words for those who struggle with the twelve-step philosophy, from one alcoholic to another. A twelve-step program uses the Twelve-Step Model. While I do not cover this information in this book, I am a proponent of the twelve steps. The steps were and are a huge part of my sobriety. They laid an incomparable foundation for my early sobriety, and I am forever connected and indebted to those who have so courageously gone before me. The twelve-step program is philosophically deep. It takes much time and patience to understand the way of committed twelve-steppers. Unfortunately, many cannot wait for the rewards and abandon the program before they have given it ample time. It is a beautiful place. Do not be afraid to return. A pureness of heart and a genuine desire will land you exactly where you need to be with the people who will best serve you.

I encourage you to open your heart. Know that you will not do best if you proceed alone. Hold the idea open. In the meantime, you have work to complete here, and I will walk you through this part of your journey.

Start Believing—Again

We question our ability to achieve newfound dreams. While this may not have been true for our whole life, it is true now. If we have been in the grip of alcoholic drinking or have been sober without trusted guidance or some type of spiritual program, we are loosely hinged. Our ability to ascertain and reveal truth has been severely compromised. Our judgment has been skewed for a long enough period of time that some of our less-healthy thinking has impaired, if not consumed, our mind. We lack the ability to trust even the simplest of processes. We criticize everything as if we already know the answer. We live in a state of paranoia, not trusting others and not trusting ourselves.

Depending on where we are in our recovery, this mind-set may, at worst, be ruling our life or merely making us neurotic. Not to worry! It can be changed. It has been programmed into us at a subconscious level, but it can be quieted over time. Begin with the idea that it is possible to change the direction of our lives. This doesn't mean that results will appear this instant. It means we have opened ourselves to the possibility that life can be different. Thinking we don't have the ability to change is what is holding us back, not the actual change. It's the thinking that's the problem. If we feel we are stuck and cannot grow, we are mistaken and not accurately informed. Living things are actually designed to prosper. It's already instilled in us at a cellular level.

Inherently, living organisms have the drive to survive. Scientifically, this term is known as the *biological imperative*. All cells (organisms) possess intelligence, and this intelligence is in communication with its environment. Science shows us that it is neither predetermined nor random. Rather, it is a two-way conversation between organism and environment. For example, a seed that falls from a tree will burrow into the soil, and its intelligent genetic design will bring forth a new, living tree. The intelligence is already within the seed. If the seed does not land in the proper environment, the intelligence will not flourish. The intelligence (seed) without the proper environment (soil, sunlight, and water) will not yield the tree. The proper environment without the seed will not yield the tree. It is the communication between the two that produces the desired result.

Humans are more complex organisms. While not as simple as the seed, we are very much the same. Our intelligence is housed in our mind. This intelligence is both our conscious mind (the mind of free will) and our subconscious mind (the mind at a cellular level). Bruce Lipton states, "We can actively *choose* how to respond to most environmental signals and whether we even want to respond at all. The conscious mind's capacity to override the subconscious mind's preprogrammed behaviors is the foundation of free will."[2] We too merge with our environment and flourish—or not. Science shows us that we are not governed solely by genetics. Our future has not already been predetermined by our DNA. Nor is it a random occurrence. Our future is based on the communication between the organism and the environment, just like the seed and the soil.

At a cellular level, our life is the product of the mixture of memory from early childhood, genetic ancestry, and past-time or historical memory. At a conscious level, we recognize our future as a longing for something different, grander, bigger, and more meaningful. It is the convergence of these two minds, conscious and subconscious, with our environment that creates the quality of our life. A redwood tree will not grow and flourish in the desert sands, but it will in the forest. Intelligence combined with environment produces the tree. Our intelligence combined with environment produces us. Like the tree, we will flourish when placed in the optimal environment. Negative, pessimistic, or unloving thinking is not the environment that will best serve us. Unfortunately, this is the environment that most of us live in by the time we decide to get sober.

When we get into a pattern of thinking, *I don't have the ability to do this work or make these changes*, we are mistaken. Based on our recent or current behavior, change may seem impossible. Based on the design and intelligence of our mind and body, it is not only possible, but probable. When placed within the proper environment with the proper mind-set, we will achieve.

We often mistake our lack of knowledge as our lack of ability. Arming ourselves with the knowledge and understanding of how to apply that information is the difference between achievers and non-achievers. We have more going for us than we realize. The fact that we don't recognize this doesn't mean it's not true. We have many capabilities, and we barely scratch the surface of them in this lifetime. Starting to alter our thinking from *Can I?* to *Show me how I can*, brings a big shift in the direction of our lives.

Feeling able to do something and believing we will actually accomplish it is one of the greatest feelings we get to have. It may not seem that way at the onset. The long and seemingly endless road can be daunting. The key is to keep glimpses of the goal fresh and to notice markers of progress along the way. Without these, we are apt to quit. The destination is sweet because we know the perseverance it took to get there. The markers are encouraging because they reinforce our belief and propel us forward. We absolutely must see that we are progressing in our endeavor. Not noticing our progress can cost us a lot. Oftentimes, the price paid is the loss of our sobriety.

At times, we confuse *speed* with actual *progress*. We think we need to get everywhere quickly. The time it takes to reach a destination does not matter. That we get there does. They are two separate parts of the equation and should not be treated as equal. When we confuse the time frame with the actual achievement, we are setting ourselves up for disappointment.

Completion dates are an important component to any goal; however, hinging our success on the date can mess with our head—especially if we don't make the deadline.

The key here is to do our best to work toward what we want. If the result doesn't come, we can take alternative action: postpone the completion date, reassess the feasibility of the goal, reset the goal, or look for the blessing and establish a new direction toward which we feel inspired to move.

Despite our perceptions, all things work out for the good in the end. If we aren't at that good place yet, it is safe to say we are not at the end. Life does have a way of working itself forward.

Seventh Challenge: Become familiar with the feeling of actually stepping through your fears. Journal about what you thought it would feel like versus how it actually felt.

Inspiration and Choice

When we feel inspired to do or achieve something, we go for it. If we're not sure that it's real inspiration, we let it sit for a while. The truth is relentless. If we are meant to do something, it will revisit our mind again and again. This constant revisiting is the way we make change in our life. We get an idea, and then it grows grander until we finally act on it. For example, if we currently own a car, it was something we once dreamt of having. As time passed, it grew closer to manifesting, and eventually it did. What we think about is what manifests. There is always a first thought. What we do with that thought determines whether or not it will manifest. That seemingly fleeting thought is actually our inspiration.

It is inspiration that appears from thin air. We're out eating pizza because we had a hankering for pizza. Where does that thought come from? We will learn about the infinite world of possibilities in Part III. For now, wherever it comes from, it is ours, and we have the choice to act on it or not.

The word *choice* requires further investigation. Our choices are based on our beliefs. Our beliefs are based on our programming and life experience. We must first become consciously aware of how we are subconsciously thinking. When we get good at seeing what lives within us subconsciously, we become masters at creating a different life. Our awareness will be the catalyst for change. And we are about to become aware.

If we don't do this work, who will? No one else can gather the courage to do what needs to be done in our lives. We are either going to get dragged through life or move through willingly. Learn to adjust to change. After all, change is the one thing that is certain. It has always been happening and will continue to happen. It cares not if we like it or are along for the ride. It's coming anyway.

We all have a natural breaking point, a place where we say, *That's enough.* Like a winter iceberg slowly melting, eventually a piece falls free and floats away. Over time, it will simply be more ocean water. It is still something; it is just no longer the iceberg. Do we see that we have been slowly melting? We are floating away from who we once were. We are ready to become something so much more—the ocean. We have a threshold. Once we pass through, we can no longer return to the way it was. The place our mind wants to take us is new and unfamiliar, so we hang on to the old. It feels secure; even if it is sick and unhealthy, at least it is predictable. When we have finally had enough, we will be willing to let go.

It is the holding on when we could be letting go that is causing our suffering.

It is our thought about the change, not the actual change, that is causing our suffering.

It is what we do with that thought, not the actual thought, that is causing our suffering.

It is our perception of not knowing how and why, not the actual how and why, that is causing our suffering.

We have free will, and we can choose to change!

Dialogue 4

<u>June 2004: Sobriety—Day 185</u>

A: *Things are definitely getting better, but not better enough. When is all this joy coming? I feel so depressed.*

B: *Life is much better than it's been in a long time, and you know it. You just don't want to admit it.*

A: *Okay. Better in some ways, but worse in others.*

B: *No, not worse. It's just that now you are aware. You weren't aware before. Somehow you think that because you weren't aware of what was going on that it wasn't happening. Now you are aware, and you get to deal with it. You get to stop running away.*

A: *Great. Aware of what? I am a creep, was a creep—am a creep.*

B: *Stay sober. You will learn, I promise.*

A: *I hate sobriety.*

B: *That's okay. No one said you had to like it. Do it anyway.*

Part III: The Essentials

Physics

In Part III of this book, we will explore the components that are required for a happy, peaceful, purposeful life. We will delve more deeply into the role that science plays in our evolution. This will be a study of what we know to be true from a scientific standpoint—data that has been proven. We will briefly explore modern physics and quantum physics. Bruce Lipton states, "Physics, after all, is the foundation for all the sciences."[1] Understanding and applying this information will be a gigantic leap toward a fulfilling present and future.

Physics is the science that deals with matter and energy and their interactions. When we think of physics, we think of things like gravity; when something falls, it goes down, not up. Physics, as we use the term in this book, is the practical interpretation of our everyday world seen with our unaided eye.

The science of quantum physics applies to the invisible world most of us will never see. It is the micro view of life and cannot be seen with the naked eye. In the quantum world, traditional physics is slightly altered. The same components are studied, but in quantum physics we learn that matter is actually energy (a vibration). The website ThinkQuest.com describes quantum physics this way:

> Quantum science is a branch of science that deals with discrete, indivisible units of energy called quanta as described by the Quantum Theory. There are five main

ideas represented in Quantum Theory: 1) Energy is not continuous, but comes in small but discrete units, 2) The elementary particles behave both like particles *and* like waves, 3) The movement of these particles is inherently random, 4) It is *physically impossible* to know both the position and the momentum of a particle at the same time. The more precisely one is known, the less precise the measurement of the other is, and 5) The atomic world is *nothing* like the world we live in.[2]

Why is learning about quantum physics important to recovery? Because we learn:

1. The value of looking beyond what the unaided human eye can see;
2. That we are interconnected in ways we do not currently comprehend;
3. That thoughts are energy and are therefore prone to the quantum theory.

When we take a closer look at these three areas, we will acquire some useful knowledge about our limiting beliefs. When we remove some of those beliefs, we can begin to live life fully.

<u>Note for the true science buff</u>: My intention is to present complex material in a simplified manner in order to reach a broad audience.

<u>Note for the scientifically challenged</u>: Stay with me. It's not as complicated as it seems in the beginning.

Beyond the Unaided Eye

The implication here is that all that exists is the stuff we can see, the actual matter, i.e., the desk, the chair. This is not true. While these things appear to be physically solid, they actually are not. At a quantum level, the particles are floating in and out of reality as we see it. This is challenging for the mind to grasp; nevertheless, it is true. Our minds reject this idea because we know that we see what we see. Quantum physics challenges these beliefs, and we do not want the world as we know it to be challenged.

Less than five hundred years ago, Copernicus challenged the science of astronomy by introducing a heliocentric system. That Earth was not the center of our universe was a notion that did not fare well during his time. Despite criticism, his idea was, in fact, true. History is riddled with similar times when we thought we knew something with certainty but found later that we did not.

The development of observational instruments has become the authority on what is. We can now view subatomic matter and can say for certain that it is unlike our understanding of classic physics. Just because we don't believe it doesn't make it any less true. After all, we believe in electricity, but very few of us have a scientific understanding of how it works. We just know it exists because, when we flip the switch, light appears. Approach these forthcoming ideas with an open mind. We are about to see ourselves in a revolutionary way.

Connected in Ways We Do Not Comprehend

It is difficult to imagine that we are all connected. We see where our body ends; we see emptiness (air); and then we see where another person's body begins. It is unfathomable that this is all connected. It doesn't look even close to being connected. How can that be?

While our individual bodies appear to end at our skin, there is an energy emitting through and from each of us. This energy extends beyond our bodies out into the field. The field is all the space around us that we do and do not see. It is one continuous vibration that does or does not bundle itself into stuff we can see with our naked eye. In our mind, this field has never existed. We can't see it; nevertheless, it is there. Compare it to air. We don't see the air, but we know that it's there. We know because we breathe. Few of us understand the science of breathing, yet all agree it is necessary if we want to sustain life. We accept it as truth, despite the fact that we do not see it.

Let's take a closer look at this field. Science has shown us that fields exist around all living things. We know it is there because we can measure the frequency of the wavelength. All living things are emitting energy, and that energy is moving through our bodies all the time. Think, for example, of your cell phone, TV, or radio reception. It arrives through a frequency in the electromagnetic field—out of thin air, so to speak. We believe it exists because we see the TV or hear a voice coming through the cell phone or radio, not because we understand the science.

The field is where everything is happening. Lynne McTaggart, author of *The Field: The Quest for the Secret Force of the Universe,* states that this field is "an open ocean of microscopic vibrations in the space between things."[3] As challenging as this is to comprehend, we are all connected in a gigantic sea of energy moving at different vibrations and frequencies. McTaggart shares, "The very underpinning of our universe was a heaving sea of energy—one vast quantum field."[4] We question how this can be possible, yet it is a fact. Our visible world is not the only world, just the one we believe in because we see it with our eyes.

In the quantum world, reality is not tangible matter but energy, vibration. And according to Einstein, "There is no place in this new kind of physics both for the field and matter, for the field is the only reality."[5] Say what? This means, simply, that it's all about the field. Matter (stuff that looks real) is really non-material; it's energy. It just appears real from our limited perspective. We can hold this book, not because it is dense matter, but because it is dense energy. Because the energy is vibrating at such a high level, it is actually creating an invisible energy force that appears solid.

Additionally, the field is everywhere. There is no such thing as *empty*. Nowhere is there a void. There is something everywhere in our universe.

What's happening in the field can be affecting us, and we can be affecting the field. What we receive and what we impart is determined by our mind. Evidence shows that the subconscious mind serves as a type of receiver and the field functions as an antenna. We send and receive based on what we believe to be true. We are aware and experience life to the degree that we perceive and are willing to receive the situation.

So, here we sit, reading this book. We have both a body and a mind. We identify ourselves within the context of both. We look a certain way (body). We have a certain mind (system of beliefs/way we view the world/ belief system). We live out our lives as particular people in particular ways through the sum of our particular beliefs.

So what does this mean for us and our sober life? We are receiving, sending, and storing this energy all the time. This energy is thought, arriving seemingly out of thin air (the field) into our minds.

Beliefs Are Energy

Thoughts are energy and subject to quantum theory. Scientists agree that all we can identify in the known universe is made up of time, space, matter, and energy. In the quantum world, matter exists, but it exists as energy. We are formed from energy. All the billions of cells in your body began as an intangible form of energy. For the purpose of applying this information, thought is energy, and thought energy creates our reality. Our person is energy. Our thoughts are energy, and our thoughts are creating our world.

Understanding and applying this information will move our lives forward. When we understand the facts behind why we behave the way we do, it is much easier to do something different. We recognize the thought for what it is—energy. We begin to see that it can be acted upon or not. Having the thought does not require that we take the action. It is universally understood that the learning process begins with thought upon which we take action, which leads to experience.

Beliefs are thoughts. Thoughts are energy. Where and how do we house this energy and information? This is the job of the subconscious mind. The mind has two seemingly separate divisions: the subconscious mind and the conscious mind. While we identify them separately, they work very much in tandem and coexist in the creation of ourselves and our lives. This essential balance of our minds is the mechanism that keeps us alive. Data gets processed and relayed to our bodies. Our bodies respond and relay information back. It is a beautiful system of nonstop communication that creates and sustains our livelihood.

The conscious is the thinking, creative mind. Physically, the conscious mind is located in the prefrontal cortex of the brain. As quoted from Bruce Lipton in *Spontaneous Evolution,* "The prefrontal cortex is the neurological platform that enables humans to realize their personal identity and experience the quality of thinking."[6] The conscious mind is that of logic and reasoning. It can either accept or reject ideas and concepts. It thinks in terms of past, present, and future. The conscious mind handles roughly 5 to 10 percent of our daily function. It is definitely not the quicker of the two minds.

The subconscious mind is the balance. In Bruce Lipton's book *The Biology of Belief* we learn, "The subconscious mind, one of the most powerful information processors known, specifically observes both the surrounding world and the body's internal awareness, reads the cues, and immediately engages previously acquired (learned) behaviors—all without the help, supervision, or even awareness of the conscious mind."[7]

The subconscious mind consists of our body's cellular intelligence and genetic memories, the balance of both instincts and learned experiences. It is strictly habitual, playing the same behavioral responses again and again. It does not differentiate between what is real and what is imagined. It perceives only the present moment. It has no sense of the past or future. It functions in the now. We eat, and it knows how to digest our food. We inhale, and it knows how to distribute the oxygen. It is a master at its job. It takes on a task, memorizes it, and then repeats it for a lifetime—a truly magnificent intelligence. Life would be too challenging if we had to think about blinking our eyes, beating our heart, breathing in air, and building blood cells. The subconscious takes on these necessary functions and orchestrates their performance.

With the subconscious mind managing the basics, the conscious mind is free to engage in creating. Our conscious mind has supplied our subconscious with data over the span of our lives. Once the data is rooted in our subconscious mind, the subconscious will not be able to change that information without additional cooperation. Once data is programmed, it stays until a new program is created. Any new program will need to override the old program at a subconscious level if the subconscious is to use the new data instinctually. We can't just think about it at a conscious level and expect it to change.

The subconscious mind is a processor that functions 1 million times faster than the conscious mind. Lipton states, "Our subconscious is running the show 95 percent of the time. Therefore our fate is actually under the control of *recorded programs,* or habits."[8] The conscious mind cannot compare to the efficiency and speed of the subconscious. We can have all the conscious willpower we want. Alone, it is not enough to propel us forward or alter our belief system. We can read positive affirmations and work on being optimistic. This will not suffice to create the change. Do we wonder why we can't alter that bad habit? Most times we can't because we are approaching it from a purely conscious perspective. Being conscious is no match for the data that has already been memorized by the subconscious. The key is to change the mind at a subconscious level. Get that changed, and we watch our lives change.

The Subconscious: Stores, Receives, Sends

The subconscious mind processes data three different ways: it stores information, it receives information, and it sends information.

We have a lifetime of stored data within our subconscious mind. We are unaware of much of it, and what we don't know is affecting the quality of our lives. Whether or not we think it doesn't matter, it does. Remember Lipton's words: "The most powerful and influential programs in the subconscious mind are the ones that were recorded first."[9] This data has been affecting the way we function, every day, all day long.

Once an idea has been programmed into the subconscious mind, it becomes the predominant response. It's as if that response (belief) gets locked in. Whether the programming serves us or not has no significance. The repository of our subconscious mind is simply that: a storage room for information. This stored information is our belief system. Once it becomes our belief, we seek to fulfill the truth of that belief. Not only do we seek to *fulfill* that truth, but we subconsciously look for ways to *reinforce* that truth. Our experiences are learned and locked until a new experience unlocks or overrides them. Then this new idea becomes the belief. We now function with this new belief with no additional thought required from our conscious mind. For addicts, the subconscious belief is what drives the repetitive, harmful behavior. It's no mystery why we can't stop when we say we want to stop. It's why we drink and drug again and again, despite the fact that we swore—*never again*—just this morning.

We have also learned that our subconscious mind carries information from generation to generation along with experiences from our current life. So, if we are wondering why we behave like our parents or grandparents, it's safe to say that it has been programmed into us at a biological level.

We have more stored in our subconscious mind than we might have realized was there, and it's running our life. Now, what are we going to do about it? Let it take over? We hope not. Wanting something new will require us to learn and apply something new. Our old thinking will not move us toward a new identity. It is necessary that we do the work—begin the journey of releasing any unwanted and non-serving beliefs. It's like removing the old program from the hard drive and installing a new one. We've been functioning with hardwired beliefs—many of which haven't been serving us well.

What can we do now? The solution is simple but not easy: We reprogram the subconscious mind. If we want to change (and presumably we do if we're reading this book), we get strongly, emotionally attached to the possibility that we *can* and *will* recover. If not, the programming in the subconscious will continue to prevail. In short, we create the change by experiencing a new emotion, which we do by taking new action. We take new action despite how we feel about taking new action. When we take a new action with a new motivation, we get a new result.

This work isn't about going back and regaining a time in our lives when old choices worked. It's about moving forward and learning to make *new* choices that work. This we learn through the simple act of trial and error. We learn what we do want because we are clear on what we don't want. When we have the experience of something new, and we see that we like it, we do daily work to sustain it. As we continue to attach ourselves to the new results, to the person we are growing into, this becomes the new belief about who we are, which then becomes who we are.

For the purpose of recovery, we are going to look at how the subconscious mind receives new data. There are two basic ways. The first is through cognitive work that involves both the conscious and subconscious working together. This includes, but is not limited to, modalities like life-coaching, twelve-step work, Voice A/Voice B journaling (similar to the dialogues in this book), counseling, daily prayer, inner-child work, and psychotherapy. The second way is to bypass the conscious mind and reach the subconscious directly. These modalities include, but are not limited to, EFT Tapping (Emotional Freedom Technique), Awakening, and ThetaHealing™.

Emotional Freedom Technique (EFT) Tapping is accomplished by tapping on specific meridian points in the body. A meridian point is a specific location along which energy travels. Tapping on these particular locations stimulates the energy within the body. Through the tapping, energy is released, and thus the body can heal itself. It is similar to what we know as acupressure.

Tapping is done with our fingertips. We begin by tapping on the outer side area (karate chop point) of our palm and from there we move to the inner eyebrow (nose bridge), the side of eye (temple area), the under eye (at cheekbone), under nose, center of chin, collarbone, underarm (at chest line) and lastly the head at the top center. While tapping on these meridian points we focus on acceptance of and resolution for the situation.

EFT Tapping is a great tool, especially for those who are new to this kind of work. It is extremely beginner-friendly, because it allows the client to focus on a negative emotion. (Most addicts can easily relate to these feelings.) While focusing on this emotion we use self-dialogue as we move through each of the nine meridian points of the body.

Before we begin the tapping sequence, we identify what negative emotion we want to focus on and how we feel about that emotion at this exact moment. Once we have identified how we feel about the emotion, we rate the feeling on a scale of zero to ten. Here is an example of a scenario for a beginner.

Negative emotion: *I hate that I have this drinking problem and that I have to deal with it.*

Rate emotion: *On a scale of zero to ten, it is a ten.*

Begin set-up dialogue and state three times: *Even though I have this drinking problem and I hate this situation, I deeply and completely accept myself and accept these feelings.*

The set-up statement is stated while tapping on the karate-chop point. After completing the karate chop tapping, we move through the remainder of the meridians five to seven times, starting from the brow and working down our body. Once we have completed the first series of taps, we re-rate our emotion. We continue tapping until we can get the number lowered. After we have done this, we can do additional tapping and program some affirming emotions. This statement may be: *I can deal with life without altering my mind* or *I have faith in my ability to grow and change.* Follow the same set-up and sequence as was done with the negative emotion.

This is the ultra-short version of tapping. For more information, contact Nick Ortner with The Tapping Solution or visit www.TheTappingSolution.com.

An Awakening is done through a Lightworker. A Lightworker, in layman's terms, is a person who brings love and light to Earth. It is a healer who believes that spiritual methods will heal our planet. A Lightworker assists us by activating our "light body" and awakening our truest nature—divine love, wisdom, and light. Our *light body* is the body that provides the blueprint for our physical body. Our light body is the way we communicate with spirit. It is the catalyst to communication between the physical world and the spiritual world. When our light body is blocked with outdated beliefs, unwanted blueprints, and unhealthy genetic coding, we are compromised and thus separated from optimum communication with spirit.

When we receive an Awakening we are aligning and connecting to higher self and our true purpose. This process is done through the cleaning and balancing of the chakras, as well as by DNA activation.

Chakras are the ethereal (immaterial) body's energy vortices. The origin of the word chakra means "wheel of light." The human body has seven major chakras. They are the root, sacral, solar plexus, heart, throat, brow, and crown chakras. Our chakras are the repositories of our emotions and attitudes toward life. Some of the energy stuck in our chakras has been experienced and locked from this current life, and some we have inherited. Regardless of how it got there, the goal is to clear it. According to Ambika Wauters, author of *The Book of Chakras: Discover the Hidden Forces Within You*, "The chakra system is a model for the flow of energy that runs through all life and through the human system. It is like a ladder that takes us from the physical realm of substance up through the workings of the higher mind and spirit, and into the realm of Divine Consciousness."[10] When these chakra energies are cleaned and balanced, we find that we are more connected and balanced. We are not so easily driven by fear. Fear is the largest component for an alcoholic to manage. Chakra clearing gives us relief.

DNA activation means we are increasing our ability to use more of our natural, Creator-given potential. DNA contains the genetic information for our cells and can be found in every cell in our bodies. It's the coding that lets us know what we have been, because it is who we have become. Basically, we look like our parents because we have their coding in our DNA. Our children will look like us because they carry our DNA. Scientists estimate that humans use only a small fraction of what is currently available. DNA activation begins the process of unlocking this untapped potential. DNA activation can produce radical shifts at a cellular level, especially for the alcoholic who is imprisoned by the idea that he will never recover.

Once we have our Awakening, we experience a greater sense of peace and an overall feeling of well-being. There is a subtlety and calmness to life that we had not previously noticed. Our emotions are felt more deeply and purely. This deepening in feeling no longer frightens us but brings joy. We now feel and experience life at a depth that was previously unattainable. Regardless of where we are in the path of sobriety, there is benefit to an Awakening. It provides a deepened connection to Earth and spirit. For more information on an Awakening, contact Alicia McNaughton at www. SeatofTheSoulMassage.com.

ThetaHealing™ is the act of achieving a conscious theta brainwave and using that brainwave to directly access the subconscious mind. There are five different types of brain waves: Delta (sleep/unconscious), Theta (imagination/hypnosis), Alpha (meditation/calm consciousness), Beta (normal state of consciousness/focused consciousness), and Gamma (hyper-alert/peak performance). We are in all brainwaves, to varying degrees, at all times. Brent Phillips, author of *Where Science Meets Spirit*, states:

> It is a common misconception that the brain has only one type of brainwave at a time. In fact, all of the brainwaves are active in the brain at all times, but at varying levels. So, the brain always has alpha waves, beta waves, theta waves, gamma waves, and delta waves simultaneously. What we really mean when we say that the brain is in a *theta brainwave* is that the theta brainwave is stronger (meaning it displays higher amplitude on an EEG) than the other brainwaves. In other words it is the dominant brainwave at that given moment.[11]

This information is important, because it shows that we do not require a hypnotic theta brainwave to achieve a waking and conscious theta brainwave. Theta brain activity is the threshold between what we know as our conscious and subconscious. It is through the theta frequency range that we reprogram our subconscious beliefs.

We can identify subconscious beliefs through a process referred to as *muscle testing*. The idea behind muscle testing is that the body's electromagnetic field becomes stronger when something resonates as "true" and weaker when something resonates as "false." While consciously we may believe something to be true, subconsciously we can find that we believe it to be false. The addict often says he wants sobriety, when in actuality he is petrified of who he would be sober. In this instance, we find that the subconscious belief overrides the conscious belief, and so we stay addicted. Consciously we hate being addicted, but subconsciously we see no alternative. Reprogramming this belief at a subconscious level is the key to creating a miracle in our life.

Once we have muscle-tested and checked our true belief, we can move forward and program something new. We get to reprogram a new belief that will not limit our ability to recover. We go into a conscious theta brainwave and access our Creator through the crown chakra (the chakra at the top of our head). The unconscious mind is commanded to co-create with the Creator for a specific purpose or intention.

Again, this is the ultra-short version of ThetaHealing™. However, it gives us an idea of how this modality works. For more information on receiving ThetaHealing™ in conjunction with recovery-coaching, go to www.CompetencyCoaching.com. To learn more about ThetaHealing™ or become a ThetaHealer™ practitioner, contact Brent Phillips at Theta Healing LA or visit www.ThetaHealingLA.com.

These three energy-healing modalities used in conjunction with cognitive work can and will produce tremendous results. I've experienced the results of the cognitive work alone and found it effective, and I've experienced the cognitive work in conjunction with direct subconscious healing. It was—and continues to be—amazing.

The cognitive work requires conscious effort on our part and willingness to journal, pray, and speak honestly with a coach, mentor, or health care professional. As we dig deeper into cognitive work, our subconscious beliefs will begin to surface, and as they do, we can start to deal with them.

Writing is one of the best tools. There are several writing techniques we can use to awaken this part of ourself. One resource is Tim Kelley's *True Purpose: 12 Strategies for Discovering the Difference You Are Meant to Make*. The book includes workable techniques for amateurs to begin getting in touch with their subconscious and thus their life's purpose. The action to take is to buy the book and actually begin to do the work. This isn't the type of stuff we read cover-to-cover and hope it sticks in our brain. An additional resource is author Byron Katie, who has written several books. *Loving What Is: Four Questions that Can Change Your Life*, is a must-read. In addition to her books, she has downloadable worksheets available directly from her site. More can be found by Byron Katie at www.TheWork.com.

These resources include words we read slowly, writing tools we practice daily, and books that we study deeply—again and again and again. Applying information requires repetitive effort on our part. We are working at shifting the subconscious mind and its limiting beliefs. Be prepared to do some digging. Be prepared to do it every day, because this is what recovery requires.

If we are working with a recovery—or life-coach, we will have assignments that are to be completed prior to the next session. If we are in a twelve-step program, we will have meetings to attend, as well as step-work to complete. If we are not familiar with various modes of prayer, we can begin by inquiring into what others do. We can learn from a specific religious practice, or we can simply seek a spiritual philosophy. *A Course in Miracles* is one type.

Last, but not least, we send information via our subconscious mind. Thoughts are energy, and we are thinking thoughts always. Even in our sleep, the subconscious mind is running. What we send is what we are thinking. If we are thinking that we will never make it sober, guess what? We're sending out energy that says we can't make it sober. The universe sends back whatever we put out (aka the law of attraction). When we begin to send out new energy, we get back new ideas.

Eighth Challenge: Notice what you are sending out with your silent thoughts. Notice what comes back. Try to spend some time digging and seeing some root beliefs that are positive about you. Focus on those for one day. Notice how you feel at the end of that day.

Repeating Old Behaviors

We are locked into repeating old behaviors at a subconscious level. Until we know this, we feel we are at fault and somehow to blame. We feel guilty and shameful, and this perpetuates our destructive behavior. Then come more shame and guilt, and we wonder why we can't stop drinking. If we are an alcoholic, we now have it programmed at a cellular, subconscious level. It's not going anywhere of its own volition. It will stay as the default program until we put in something new. The subconscious mind has to prevail. That is its function. The biological imperative is survival, and to our body, survival is alcohol. This is why we drink, day after day, despite the fact that we have sworn it off for good—or at least until the weekend.

Addicts understand each other's heartache. With every fiber of our being, we are going to change our drinking behaviors. We know drinking is wrong. We understand it isn't working anymore, at least most of the time. We get that we have a problem with drinking. We are clear on the fact that it is hurting those around us. We sort of know we should stop. We think we could have a problem. We want to stop, but we can't. We swear to stop—but we just can't. Yes, we can. We just have to *make the choice* to change.

Bridging these two minds is infinitely more complex than I have stated, but this is the simplest form for the average alcoholic to understand. The application for those of us who have struggled with addiction is this: we have conditioned the subconscious mind to accept our addiction and have reinforced it on physiological and emotional levels. Our addictive behavior is ingrained in the core of our being. If we are going to untangle its hold on us, we'd better be prepared for the most challenging undertaking of our life. Getting and staying sober will be one of the most demanding ventures we have ever encountered. There isn't a reference point for comparison. The consensus among those who have done it successfully is that it is the most challenging—and most rewarding—feat of a lifetime. It also contains more unknowns than most alcoholics are willing to conquer. It is brand new territory, with little to no understanding of how we will possibly achieve what it is we say (we think) we (might) want.

So here we are, getting some understanding about our addiction. We're learning about our mind and how it functions. We now have some understanding of how our mind stores, receives, and sends information—some of which we wish it hadn't stored. Nevertheless, it's there, and we get to do something about it or not. It's our choice. Biologically, we were built to survive. Lipton states in his work, "On an unconscious level, our efforts to serve as Earth stewards are driven by deeper, more fundamental programming known as the *biological imperative*—the drive to survive."[12] This is what our body will try to do for as long as it can sustain the abuse. If we don't like what's in our subconscious mind, we get to do something about it: write a new program.

For the sake of argument, let's just say that we fully understand and agree with the fact that we are an alcoholic, addicted. Intellectually knowing that we are an alcoholic will not be enough to make the transformation. Resolution alone will not be enough. The subconscious is too strong to buy into one conscious moment of *I really, really want to change this time*. Our dialogue can be compared to a conversation between us and the voice-mail message we pick up. There's no one there. It's a recording. All the talking we do won't matter. The voice-mail message can't hear us. The subconscious mind is the equivalent of a voice mail that was left thirty years ago, one that we continue to try to engage in conversation. We can get angry at the voice mail, judge the voice mail, tell the voice mail what it should be doing, but it simply doesn't matter. The recording is the recording, and it will stay that way until it is changed. And this requires action. Are we ready to take an inquiring look?

This is what we learn from self inquiry: 1) Our subconscious mind is running the show; it would behoove us to know what it is saying, 2)

Willpower alone is not enough to change any habit, 3) We can't make it alone without help, and 4) Our thoughts are a type of energy and therefore programmable.

Act Different . . . How?

Let's say we're driving, and the radio is playing a song we don't like. What do we do? Push the button and change it. Simple. Someone taught us how to reach out and change the button. Our brain is hardwired to move our body, arm, and finger, and it takes but a second or less to reach and touch a button or a screen. We quickly and easily move our eyes for an instant, touch the button, and return to driving—all of this with very little conscious thought. It seems to happen automatically. The key here is that all of this behavior was learned, and now it is happening with what seems like very little effort. The truth is that it took a long time for us to learn most of these motor skills. It also took hundreds of hours of driving to learn to be a competent driver. While most of our basic function was programmed early on, we continue to program and reinforce new ideas all the time.

If we are reading this book, we are presumably at a juncture where we want to do something different—a humble and yet admirable starting point. Just because we have failed before does not mean we are fated for failure. We can look at it as being one step closer to finally reaching our goal. Edison said, "If I find ten thousand ways something won't work, I haven't failed. I am not discouraged, because every wrong attempt discarded is another step forward."[13]

If we haven't been successful the way we had hoped, we needn't be discouraged. We now have an overflowing information bank of what not to do. Now we can begin to draw on it and allow it to help us move forward. Don't be afraid of past failure. It is a necessary step toward achievement. Nobody does life perfectly. Nobody.

Getting into action when our mind is screaming *no* is a gut-wrenching experience. If we are feeling like a hostage in our own head, we can be assured that it is the normal outcome to our disconnected life. Most of us have experienced this type of agony. I have done plenty wrong as I journeyed to a new identity. What I have never done, however, is quit. I have followed the simplicity of these key competencies and have found the summit easier to climb. I have survived my completely deranged thinking and traded it in for something more reasonable, more manageable.

Part IV: The Competencies

The word *competency* comes from the root word *competent* which means *having the capacity to function or develop in a particular way.*[1] *Competent* is "derived from the Latin word *competentia,* meaning 'meeting together, agreement, symmetry.'"[2] Being competent declares that we are capable. At first, we may only be able to do something moderately, slightly, or not at all. Over time, with repetition, we are able to master a task.

Learning about competency is one thing. Learning to embody competency is quite another. Learning about something means we can repeat it on cue. We have memorized it. *Embodying* means that we function naturally at a subconscious level. It is who we have become. We have not only learned what it takes to become this person, we have also displayed this behavior in our actions for an extended period of time. Our words match our actions, and we can now say we possess the quality of integrity. Integrity means:

- we have decided who we want to be;
- we have worked hard at becoming that person;
- we can now say that this is who we are, and it is true;
- others now know that this is true; and
- our word is good to others and to ourself.

When our word is accurate to ourself, then our word is accurate to others. Trust for self eventually brings trust for others. We either want to be a certain thing—or not. We have either worked hard to achieve something—or not. We can say with certainty that this is who we are—or not. Our word is either good—or not. When we choose to live with integrity, it means that our word matters, even when no one is looking, even when there is something at risk, and even if we made a mistake. Integrity is not the by-product of thinking we are something, but the result of actually being something worth being. We cannot solely think our way into being a person others trust. We must act our way into being someone that others trust. We must first start with acting like someone *we* trust.

Somehow along the way, it became okay to be dishonest with ourselves. No one else was going to find out, so it seemed all right to cheat a little. We rationalized our behavior. After a time, we got comfortable not keeping our promises to ourselves. It felt normal. Soon it became easier to not keep promises to others. They got a little upset, but not that mad. It was certainly bearable. Yes, it was all bearable. This became the new routine, and it was okay that we didn't trust ourselves and that others didn't really trust us either. After all, life was just plain hard.

We believed that if other people's lives were as hard as ours, they'd have behaved the way we did. So we moved through life with this idea that we had it bad, and others could not possibly understand. We thought it was normal, and we came to accept it as who we were. We embodied this false philosophy. We adapted to the idea that life was just hard. Life wasn't fair. Our parents screwed us up. What was the point in trying when it was futile? We moved forward in life with these beliefs and never bothered to investigate if they were true. We didn't even know *how* to investigate our own thinking. We had deceived ourselves for so long, it appeared to be the only way. It never occurred to us that it could be any different. As a matter of fact, when someone told us it could be different, we thought they were crazy. We did not believe or trust others.

Locked into this frame of thinking only produces more of the same. After all, the subconscious seeks to reinforce its programming. We will need to shatter our old identity if this is to change. We demolish the old identity by acting our way into a new identity. It is painful, horribly painful. It is the hardest thing we will ever do, and worse yet, we have no reference point for how we are going to do it. Nor do we know others who have done it. We have not walked through anything like this before. As hard as it may seem, it is still easier than staying where we are.

We must not fear making the change; we must fear staying the same. When faced with the option, the horror of staying the same is too much to bear. It is then that we are ready to change.

Development of Five Key Competencies

As we proceed to the key competencies of long-term sobriety, we may have a tendency to become overwhelmed. These are skills that will be acquired a little at a time. They are mind-sets that will take us years to master. The most important idea is that we don't quit, which has therefore earned its place in the number one spot.

Key competencies to a sober identity:
1. I am determined.
2. I am straightforward.
3. I can be navigated.
4. I can reframe my perspective.
5. I can evolve.

Competency One: I am determined.

We are given the gift of choice. Begin to use it. We are not a victim of alcoholism.

Determination is the act of definitely deciding. We have a fixed intention of achieving a desired goal. Determination is the core of both small and great achievements. It is a settling of the mind on the firmness of our commitment. Hurdles will appear; this is a given. Wanting something and focusing on acquiring it does not mean it will come without an exchange. When we are determined, there is no trade we aren't prepared to make. We are like water, forever on course. We don't need to force our way but simply recognize the barrier and flow around it, over it, under it, or through it. The hindrance never stops us, only slows us. We recognize that the objections in our mind are there from programming. They are not real; they are only our initial reaction to the obstacle. The reaction is the first thought that happens instinctually, automatically. We learn that reacting is not the same as responding. Now when we respond, we experience a measure of thought before we speak or act. We recognize that we are placing a new belief system into place. This new system requires a moment to weigh our options before we proceed.

Until now, the favored position has been one of quitting, laziness, or indifference. The least amount of effort required has been all that has been put forth. Once or twice, we may have applied more energy, but it was met with resistance, so we concluded that trying does not work and only produces a false sense of hope. Trying only works, however, if we are determined to try until we get it right. If the goal is to try and not to achieve, we are cutting ourself short on receiving the reward we most desire. It's never enough to know that we tried once or twice and failed, especially if it is something we say we want. The question now becomes this: Do we really want the things we say we want, or do we just want to *say* that we want them? For many, this is shocking. We have been walking around, not achieving much of anything, while trying to accomplish everything. We feel slighted by others and often slighted by a universe that seems unloving and unfair.

Don't over-think it; experience it. The difficulty comes when we see there is still room to maneuver, still time to talk ourselves out of the agreement. And this is what the mind wants to do. The subconscious mind will convince us that it's not that bad the way it is, that we're okay, that we can make it one more day and change any bad behaviors tomorrow! Unless we are in a sufficient amount of pain, the catalyst for change may not be great enough. It is in this pain-filled mind-set that we become determined and driven to succeed. The initial burst of energy to transcend any behavior is easy. It usually shows up within minutes or hours after a catastrophe has occurred. It's easy to be determined then. There appears more at stake at these moments. More than was previously apparent to us.

That mess has been there all along, slowly evolving. We never noticed the severity of it, so we never sought a solution. The challenge is to see the bigger picture, to start growing because we want to take control of our life, because we want something more than we've ever wanted anything before. It is our moment, and we are ready to step in, regardless of the cost. Waiting for severe pain has been the habit. We no longer want that to be the starting point of something good. It is simply too harsh and certainly unnecessary.

Making the shift to a determined mind-set is the hardest step. The shift doesn't come while we're entertaining the idea of jumping. Nor does it come once we've jumped. It arrives in the sliver of time when we stop thinking about it and just do it. It's the void we create in our minds when we realize that, alone, we do not have the answer. When there is an opening, a new thought will appear. It can't *not* happen. We release to the moment, and the universe responds.

Being determined has more than sobriety wrapped around it. What we are talking about here is our life—*the quality of our whole life*. What do we want it to be? This goes way beyond not being an addict. It becomes our mission in life. We've always had a mission. Only we can identify what it is and how best to achieve it. We have more power than we know. We just haven't known how to orchestrate our talents and move through our challenges. We have accepted quitting as the norm. Something more in our life will require something more from us. It is time to dig deeper.

Competency Two: I am straightforward.

Being straightforward is about honesty. Stop hiding from the truth. It will pursue us relentlessly.

Being straightforward means we tell the truth, to the best of our ability. We do not camouflage it with a hidden agenda. We learn what we want, and we learn to ask for help. We have learned that sometimes we get what we want through an avenue that appears as *I-guess-this-is-what-I-needed.*

We know how to tell others *yes* as well as *no*. We are clear on who we are becoming. We are not prone to gossip. We do not speak words that are unproductive. We are kind to people, not just the ones we like. We know what it feels like to understand and express our knowledge or feeling on a subject. We can present ideas without anger and argument. We begin to see the places where we cut corners and play small. We see that in the past we'd rather walk away from the challenge of sobriety than face it. We are willing to see where we have lied and omitted the truth. We remember past mistakes because we do not want to repeat past behaviors. We focus on how we are behaving today. We don't lie to ourselves about how we are behaving.

If we find that we have lied, we work on stopping next time. If we are in the middle of a lie, we can stop and pause a moment. We can stop the lie in mid-sentence. And yes, we will lie again. We will do it until we no longer see the value in doing it. It will no longer be a thought to lie or not to lie. We will simply move toward honesty because that is who we are becoming. Yes, in the beginning it will require discipline, but eventually it will take little effort to say what is real and true. The problem until now is that we have wanted telling the truth to come easily. It never does for a chronic liar. Lying is another bad habit we have programmed into our person. For many, the ordinary task of opening our mouths means a lie is forthcoming. It takes hundreds of tries before we are able to stop the lies. And then, after much perseverance, telling the truth will seem easier.

The pattern for us has been to work the situation by blaming someone else. Even if we knew we would eventually get caught, the delayed consequences were always preferred. Any amount of pain or confrontation was best dealt with later. In dealing with it later, we could somehow make someone else feel wrong. In one way or another, it was never our fault. We were a master at making others feel guilty. We were positively unstoppable when it came to lying and weaving a story. We were so good at deception that we believed our own lies. The line between what was truth and what was non-truth had long ago been erased. The boundary was gone, and we did not care. All that we wanted was to come out clean and shiny, even if it was at another's expense. We thought little of others, and then only if they could serve us. Our motives were always self-seeking. Even when we thought we were being genuine and caring, we had an agenda: to get the other person to like us again or maybe even trust us.

All the while, we secretly hated ourselves, even though we would not admit that for a long, long time. We had no reference point for being genuine or earnest, and we didn't have a clue where to begin. Being straightforward meant being mean and bulldozing. We didn't care too much about others' feelings. Why should we? We were stuck with emotions we did not know how to handle. Being appropriate, thoughtful, and of service were words that eluded us. It was hard to let others see us, because we didn't know who we were. We were not going to let our guard down and have someone see that we didn't know ourselves. That kind of vulnerability was for the weak. We did not want to see that we were weak. We especially did not want others to see our weakness. So, rather than be vulnerable, we lied. We didn't consciously think it at the time. What we were thinking was that we were protecting ourselves. We had to do it that way. It went that way for so long that we finally became a person who lied and manipulated. The lies were knotted and coiled. We pulled the knots tighter because we kept on lying.

To be straightforward means that we know and care about ourselves, and we seek to understand and care about others. We use our words with sincerity. We see that when we gain, everyone gains; when we are self-seeking, everyone loses. Today we know what it's like to feel clean inside. We are no longer hiding. We are learning to be okay with being us. Even those things we don't prefer, we can work on growing and changing; and in the meantime, we can still love ourselves and see that we are doing our best. We are determined to live a better life each day.

Competency Three: I can be navigated.

Navigation is about guidance. We are willing to trust in a new source. We are willing to learn how that source feels.

The early explorers used navigational tools to reach the new land. We too require tools to pilot our journey. Heading out on any venture alone and unprepared is foolish. Most of us wouldn't take a trip unless we had researched our destination. Once we had decided where to go, we would never leave the directions to chance. We would have Googled the directions and plugged them into our cell phone or GPS, or at least scribbled some notes. We already know that we don't know how to get to a new place without direction. And we know that there are resources that do. We don't think twice about consulting them and following their suggested directions.

Why, then, do we embark on the journey of our sober life with so little understanding of our resources? How did we expect to arrive there? It seems we have left much to chance or fate. We are lost, yet puzzled as to why. This suggests we have accepted the role of victim without even realizing it.

There are three main parts to this competency: to ask for, to receive, and to act upon guidance. The first implies that there is someone or something to ask, that there are sources of information that can be supplied to help us maneuver. To receive help indicates that, once we have asked, we are willing to hear what this resource gives us. We receive it as if receiving a gift, with gratitude. Finally, acting upon guidance completes this competency. It means we are willing to try something new, something utterly unfamiliar, because somewhere in our being, it seems like it is the best thing to do.

This is a challenging competency. We have our belief system rooted in the presumed fact that we are alone, we've always been alone, and we will always be alone. It is far-reaching to see that we are not only loved but that there are people and resources to support us as we journey. We often feel we have tapped out our reserves. We have not. We have barely opened the box of support that will carry us through. Where does this help come from? It's all around us.

Here are some of the resources I found. They come in four basic categories: people, organizations, literature/books, and other. Regardless of where we are guided, be certain our source has understanding of addiction or can lead us to someone with knowledge on addiction.

<u>People</u>

1. Life Coach/Recovery Coach: A coach is someone who can help us work on discovering and achieving goals. Similar to a sports coach, he or she helps us look at our current skill level and trains us in the art of achieving a particular outcome. "Life coach" and "recovery coach" are not necessarily synonymous. Search for a coach who is familiar with (and has preferably walked through) addiction. Additionally, there are life coaches who specialize in childhood trauma, abuse, eating disorders, and body image.

2. Spiritual Healer/Lightworker: Spiritual healers or lightworkers are licensed therapists who work specifically with holistic healing techniques. They can also be referred to as holistic healers. They do what is commonly referred to as energy work, which includes: Awakenings, Reiki, chakra-balancing, energetic bodywork, and crystal healing.

3. EFT Practitioner: An energy healer that works with the meridians in the body for healing at a subconscious level. Tapping and dialogue are facilitated through a practitioner.

4. ThetaHealer™: A theta healer is a certified and licensed practitioner of ThetaHealing™. He or she uses a technique of achieving a conscious theta brainwave to access the subconscious mind.

5. Therapist: A therapist is a person who is trained in methods of treatment and rehabilitation that do not involve the use of medication. Many therapists specialize in addiction. Many are recovered addicts themselves.

6. Psychiatrist: A psychiatrist is a medical doctor who is licensed to prescribe medication and works in the branch of medicine that deals with mental, emotional, or behavioral disorders. When working with a psychiatrist, let him or her know that we are a recovering addict.

7. Mentor: A mentor is, in its simplest context, a trusted counselor. This is a person who has our best interests at heart. He or she can be a family member, a family friend, a clergyman, or a school counselor. It must be someone we feel we can trust and respect.

While we may not work with this person long-term, he or she is available to introduce us to newer resources.

Organizations
1. Twelve-step groups (AA, NA, PA, etc.)
2. Women's/men's groups (Check local listings under "therapist.")
3. Online support groups (Google search, i.e., IntheRooms.com)
4. Spiritual groups or religious organizations (Check local listings under "churches" or "synagogues")

Literature/Books
Reading expands our minds because, for those moments, we are pulled into the author's world. It can be a pleasant reprieve from the inner machinations of our own minds. Self-help books are wonderful; however, we should not limit our genre choice. We are gaining wisdom whenever we willingly receive a new perspective to our old and all-too-familiar story. Read in genres of spirituality, fiction, poetry, science, history, philosophy, and metaphysics. For a specific list of books, see the Suggested Reading section of this book.

Other
Additional information on all these resources can be located in the Resources section of this book.
1. Become a student of a new philosophy, e.g., *A Course In Miracles*. This course is a thoughtful and challenging example of what can be studied. For an introduction to *ACIM,* look for books authored by Marianne Williamson.
2. EFT Tapping (Emotional Freedom Technique): Also known as Meridian Tapping Technique (MTT) or just Tapping, EFT Tapping is an energy therapy. The idea is that the tapping uses the ancient meridian system to relieve stress and pain. It balances the energy system with a gentle tapping procedure that stimulates the designated meridian end points on the face and body. Tapping is

a newer energy-healing modality. We are still learning about its full benefits.

3. Audio books: This would be any book we desire to read that we can get on audio. If we are going to fill our minds with something, it might as well be something that is helping us evolve as human beings.

4. Meditation: This is the act of engaging in contemplation or reflection. It is a mental exercise that involves disciplining the mind. We can concentrate on a mantra or simply on our breathing. The purpose of meditation is to reach a heightened sense of spiritual awareness.

5. Prayer: To pray is to address or petition a Source greater than oneself. For some, this is God; for others, it can be a higher self (a self within), a Creator, or a Source. There is more than one path to this Source. What is most important is that the petition be made and that it be made in earnest.

6. Yoga: A type of exercise. In American culture, it is primarily used for attaining physical and mental control and well-being. Yoga is also a theistic philosophical teaching in which the higher self is seen as distinct from the activity of the mind, body, and will.

7. An Awakening: Done with the assistance of a lightworker, this resource is used for accessing our light-body and awakening within us our truest nature: love, wisdom, and light. Things that can happen during an Awakening include: awareness of our true purpose on earth; realignment of the mind, body, and soul; clearing of fear patterns that may be causing destruction at a cellular level; and DNA activation (changing the messages that are sent to our DNA).

8. Daily exercise or concentrated movement: Volumes have been written on the advantages of exercise. This is no mystery; at least it shouldn't be, if we have been paying attention. Exercise strengthens our body. It also increases our endorphin production, which in turn facilitates mental and physical balance.

9. Massage: This is the movement of the body tissue through manipulation (effleurage, kneading, or rubbing). Whether done with hands or an instrument, it has therapeutic effects. Massage can induce endorphin production.

10. Journaling: There are several methods of journaling: writing from a self-help workbook, free-form journaling, Voice A/Voice B journaling (similar to the dialogues in this book), and writing-to-receive-an-answer journaling. All journaling is effective because it takes our thoughts and removes them from our heads as well as helps us filter through them once on paper.

11. Healing Music: Sound that is balancing, relaxing, and peaceful. Most New Age music falls into this category. We just need to sample different types and see what resonates. Sources for sampling can be found online.

At this juncture in our lives, we may only have a limited circle of people or other resources at our immediate disposal. Some of the resources we do have are either not healthy for us or are irritated with us. Unhealthy resources will get weaned as we grow. Over time, we will want to release old ties that pull us down, not because we are angry but because we have decided it is time to move on. This can be difficult, as we see these old ties as allies. It is hard to let go of something (or someone) we think supports us. The universe understands and will not leave that space void; something or someone new will quickly move in. The challenge will be to encourage and recognize that new resource. At first we may not, and this is where our life coach, mentor, or twelve-step sponsor can be extremely beneficial. They will help us reframe our thinking in ways that are nearly impossible to do on our own.

So, now that we have asked, new information is arriving. What do we do with it? Up until now, we've not trusted anyone. To receive, we have to extend a measure of trust that previously was not there. We start with something simple. If a trusted resource suggests we make our bed daily—we do it. If we are already doing this, we do the opposite. The idea is to start following a suggestion and doing something different from what we have been doing.

Getting inspired or directed to completely stop judging others is not an accomplishable first goal. We must start with tasks that are doable and move out of our comfort zone. Never follow through with anything that isn't in alignment with the Golden Rule; in other words, don't do anything to another person that we wouldn't want done to us. When in doubt, ask another trusted source. Our own thinking has us in our current position. Without contrary ideas, we will not yield a new result. Start small. Notice successes. Move on to bigger challenges.

This brings us to the third leg of navigation: to act upon guidance. Since guidance shows up in so many different ways, it is not always easy to decipher guidance from manipulation. A good standard would be this: if it is a loving thought for self and for others, it will be a good action. Now we might be thinking, how can making or not making our bed be a loving or unloving idea? It is loving because, if we haven't been doing it, we will learn the virtue of discipline, and if we *have* been doing it, we will learn the virtue of accepting new ideas.

Anytime we take on a new task, we learn the advantage of doing work, despite how we feel about it. This is a quality that will serve us well in life. It's not about making the bed or not making the bed. It's about being willing to do things differently from how we have been doing them and being willing to develop a framework for change. As addicts, we have been used to the quick, quicker, quickest of satisfactions. We want what we want when we want it. We don't want to do things that don't feel good, so we blow off responsibilities and people. We have not yet learned that life is not always comfortable. We have sought pleasure first. We are ill-equipped to handle the basic discomforts of life. Any hardship is another excuse to drink. The goal in acting on guidance is that we learn there are many ways to handle problems. Disciplining our minds allows us to think more clearly and slowly. We now look for the best-thought-out answer, not the quick one.

We've all felt inspiration. It shows up as an idea out of nowhere. At its simplest level, it is something like having the thought: *Fold the laundry.*

Now, folding the laundry is not cause for distress. However, stranger tasks have sent alcoholics to the liquor store. What happens if we let this small inspiration go unnoticed? We delay, feel guilty, delay, still feel guilty, add more delay, and inevitably more feeling guilty. Eventually, we think about the load of clothes in the washer. Postponement of folding those in the dryer has left this next load molding, and all because we refused to act on the inspiration to fold the clothes. And so the drama continues. We need what is in the dryer to wear to work tomorrow, the kids' soccer uniforms have yet to get into the machine at all, and their game is tonight—no, in two hours! Oh, well, they can wear them dirty, and we'll need to find something else to wear tomorrow. And all the while, we're wondering why we are such a loser. The anxiety is too much. What to do? What to do? Have a drink, get mad, blame someone else, or blow it off altogether. Who needs to be accountable anyway?

And so it goes this way with every little idea, day after day, ignoring those soft reminders that keep life calmer. We receive ideas and inspirations all the time and spend most of our time arguing with them. We secretly love the chaos. It makes us feel alive. It makes everyone else crazy, and we don't even see it. We have been programmed for mayhem. It's what we know. We recreate it—constantly. Then we wonder why things never seem to change for us. They never change because *we* never change.

The objective of our ability to act upon guidance is the next step in making some permanent shifts in our identity. Whether it is the suggestion of a trusted friend, life coach, family member, or a song on the radio, we can view it without bias. We look for the possibility of how it can work, how it might work, or how it will help.

When we ask for guidance, we are simply saying we don't know or we are not clear on which way to go. It is a measure of humility. When we receive, we are showing that we are open to guidance, to another's perspective. When we act on this information, we are at the first stage of impressing a new model into our subconscious mind. The action moves us to a knowing, an undeniable truth. We know it is true because we have experienced its truth.

It's like saying the words, *I'm sorry.* Where there was anger, there is now freedom, and we can't even explain why, because absolutely nothing has changed except our mind.

It is admirable to read, to get inspired and motivated. However, if we don't apply new knowledge, it is useless. All the pondering in the world will change nothing if we do not take action. Thinking by itself accomplishes nothing. What we require is experience. Experience comes via action.

To say, *I can be navigated,* means we don't know the answer, and we are willing to ask a trusted source. It means we openly listen for a possible solution. Lastly, the new information moves beyond the mind and becomes an action we take. There is no guarantee that this will be the absolute answer. However, our asking for guidance is an indication that we are willing to move in a new direction. Any movement is better than no movement. As it's often said, "Imperfect action is better than no action."

Competency Four: I can reframe my perspective.

Reframing has two parts. We reframe to see the situation from a new angle. We reframe to grant pardon and experience forgiveness.

Seeing from a New Angle
Many regard their perspectives as absolute truth, as factual. This is not so. Truth is not determined by the number of people who believe it. Truth just is. We can work our hardest to convince others that we are right, but that doesn't make it so. Rather, we are manipulating or persuading others to conform to our way of thinking. Our preferred stance has been that others either agree with our point of view or they were wrong. It is unfathomable to us that we might be seeing something erroneously. It is impossible that we have it wrong. Even more challenging is the idea that the other person might actually have it right. This is so foreign to our thinking that we are in shock when we realize how far off-target we have been.

To *reframe* means being willing to look from a different angle with different eyes. It could be that we are partially right or not right at all. Either way, we are willing to look. If we have spent a lifetime being the one with all the correct answers, this competency will be enlightening for us. We will be challenged many times before we learn the value of sight from a shifted perspective.

We are as interdependent upon nature as we are upon each other. All life must coexist if it is to exist at all and flourish. Our personal relationships are no different. Until we see the value and balance of life and people, we will be caught in our own whirlwind of an existence. We will wreak havoc on anything in our path and leave behind a devastated landscape. Then, when we have calmed down, we look back and wonder why everyone is so upset. After all, we didn't really mean to do it.

It's as if we practice ethical principles by twisting them to our own warped minds and then question why others don't agree or understand. Perhaps we have experienced someone asking for our help, and we agreed; but we only wanted to do what we wanted to do to help, not what they requested. Guess what. We weren't helping. We were *pretending* to help. We were doing what we wanted to do. We were doing what was convenient for us and not what was helpful to them. Then, when they didn't want what we had to offer, we got miffed, as if we had really gone out of our way to help. We never actually helped at all, just offered what we wanted. We hate being put out, don't we? We take something so simple and make it so complicated.

Reframe is a nice way of saying, "I have it distorted in my head, and I'm willing to see where I am mistaken." Being wrong isn't something we like. It's not something anyone likes. However, saying we are never wrong is the equivalent of saying we are 100 percent right. We don't know anyone who fits this description.

Embarking on a life of reframing is a rewarding competency. Initially, we will begin reframing almost out of sheer force. It will seem alien, like learning a new language. Only through repetition will we reap the rewards. This competency requires the exerted effort of determination. It will not come with only a try or two. It requires continued effort for an extended period of time. What was initially feigned will become a most valuable asset: our ability to see the situations through simultaneous perspectives. We will no longer be the one rocking the boat, but the one keeping it steady and afloat. We will no longer be seeking to compete for others' attention or accolades. We will search rather to find a cooperative solution, one that honors the greatest good for all involved. We now have a sense of who we are.

<u>Forgiveness</u>

As children we learned that forgiveness was something God did or did not grant, depending on the earnestness of our "Sorry." Or it was something we were required to do at our parent's request. Or we genuinely wanted to forgive because we were undeniably sorry for the action we had taken. Or we wanted to grant forgiveness because what had happened was just—well, forgivable. Suffice it to say, this idea of forgiveness has presented hurdles as we have moved through recovery. Time spent contemplating wrongs and issues of worthiness, as well as understanding genuine forgiveness, has taken us a lifetime to understand. What once seemed imbalanced now makes sense. Here are the principles that we apply to our life today.

Forgiveness isn't only an action. It is a shift in our perception. It means we have mentally revisited a situation; we now empathize with another person and comprehend what he or she has done. We see their path of thought and how they arrived at the decision they chose. It doesn't mean that what they did was okay or not okay. It means we can now observe the situation without condemning it. When we judge what another has done as right or wrong, we set our standards as the bar for human behavior. We function best when we act in accordance with our own philosophy, not other people's philosophies. Others are acting in accordance with their own philosophies, not ours. We needn't worry about agreeing with them, only about acting in accordance with ours. As addicts, we are accustomed to being prone to hypocrisy. We say one thing, do another, and pretend it's all okay. When we notice that someone might not be acting in accordance with his philosophy (hypocrisy), we remember that we have not always been in alignment with our philosophy. From this place, we can let it go and not judge.

Forgiveness is something we do for ourselves so that we don't have to live each day being angry with another person. If we are angry and condemn others, we become an angry and condemning person to be around. We are, in actuality, creating reasons for others to not want to be around us. We perpetuate a situation that we disapprove of. Sadly, we believe this is justified. We will withhold our love and understanding until others realize how much they have wronged us—as if not forgiving them will teach them some kind of lesson. All the while, our unforgiveness is teaching them nothing, but it is ripping us up inside.

We all want to be the recipient of forgiveness when we are sorry. It is painful when we feel this hasn't or won't be granted. From the receiving end, the grief of not being forgiven is unparalleled; we are disappointed in both ourselves and our behavior, and we feel unworthy of forgiveness. From this point, we slip into "if only" thinking. We get stuck in the past, unable to see what might be gained. We live that moment over and over in our mind as if thinking about it will somehow change what has happened. It does not. It only prolongs the misery. We are puzzled. What we have erroneously learned is that forgiveness is not granted us, nor do we need to grant it to another. It is no mystery why we are at war within our own heads. The world preaches one set of ethics and acts on a separate set. We learn to accept this paradigm as normal. It might be normal, but it is far from sane. If we are to remain sober, we will need to grant that which we wish to receive, regardless of what was done.

Forgiveness does not mean we let someone harmful stay or come back into our life. We just let them go without judgment. Forgiveness doesn't mean that what they did was fair. Rather, we rise above it and are willing to move forward with our life. Forgiveness doesn't mean we need to pretend it didn't happen. It just means we stop obsessing on the fact that it *did* happen. Forgiveness doesn't mean we will never think of it again. The thought will come again and again, but it will have no power over us. If it does have a moment of power, we investigate our thinking. Byron Katie defines forgiveness best: "What you thought happened, didn't."[3] What this means is that when we truly forgive, we see the situation so differently that is does not even resemble what we originally thought it to be.

Forgiveness for ourselves is no different from forgiveness for others. Learning to forgive ourselves comes before learning to forgive others. If we have extended a measure of forgiveness to another, it is because we have learned to extend that measure to ourself. We cannot give something we do not possess; we cannot give a dollar if we do not possess a dollar. We cannot give our understanding if we do not possess understanding. The way we treat ourself is the way we treat others. We first have the task of seeing where we can experience compassion and understanding for our egregious behaviors.

We know we are sorry because, if we could do it again—differently—we would. Being sorry means that we wish it hadn't happened. If we don't care that it happened, we aren't sorry. The implication is that if the situation arose again, we would make a different choice. The question is, how many times have we said we were sorry only to repeat the behavior again? This is more like *we wish we were sorry*, but we're not because we want what we want without consequences. What we want is more important than others and their needs. When we have treated people this way for a prolonged period of time, it is not only difficult for them to see us differently, but overwhelmingly challenging for us to see ourselves differently. We are all locked into the old pattern.

As we begin to act in new ways, we begin to build trust with self. There comes a time when we see ourselves in earnest. Our words now have meaning for us. Others now share this perspective through both our actions and words. This fuels our sense of forgiveness. We begin to see that maybe we could learn to forgive ourselves more fully, and thus the circle of giving extends to self. We can give to ourselves, and we can give to others; there is symmetry. We have developed a competency. As time passes, we acquire an understanding of the balance in our relationships. We work on self first because we need to be good with the person we are becoming. This is the ultimate gift to those we love. We give them a person who is whole. Learning to trust ourself will be the catalyst to a life well lived. It starts with forgiveness and a genuine desire to do better.

When we extend forgiveness to another, we have given it to ourself first. We reap the reward because we are no longer captive within our mind. While this may be challenging at first, the long-term effects are extraordinary. At first we may be wondering why everything feels so boring, kind of regular with no drama going on. Over time, we will crave the sweet silence and lightly question how we managed to get along without it. The truth is, we did not manage to get along without it. Our life was chaos. It took our life getting quiet to see how noisy it was. When we were in the noisy room, it seemed normal. Now it is extremely burdensome to hold on when we could be letting go. We have learned the power of forgiveness, and when we change our mind, somehow our body follows right along. It's nice to feel content within our own skin. It's a gift we had never known.

How do we know it is time to reframe our thinking? We know because we hurt inside. Something just doesn't set right. Sometimes we can put our finger on it; sometimes we can't. Either way, we have learned that our discomfort is from within, not from without. After all, we are the only one in our head. That other person is nowhere in sight, and we're mad at them.

We suffer as we silently reiterate the miserable story. Not only do we hit the replay button for ourself but for anyone who will listen. We are reinforcing how right we are and how wrong they are. This is how we hold onto our anger: we decide another is at fault. We live in this space as if it has meaning and purpose. It has neither. It is an illusion of control. The freedom we seek comes from letting it go, releasing it. There is no other way. We cannot grab hold of a new perspective until we have released the old perspective.

Life is really one extended reframe. It is the exchange of our current truth for a different truth. We never appreciated our parents until we had children of our own. We grumbled about running when we were tired until we couldn't go because it was raining too hard. We adopted an attitude that whatever we had was not what we wanted. The truth is, we had exactly what we needed. We just didn't see it. We were unaware that we already possessed all that we required. What we lacked was recognition and appreciation. What was missing was our ability to see from a different angle. The only thing that is ever missing in a situation is what we are not bringing. A shift in our perception is the difference between abundance and lack. We hold the key to the way we choose to see.

Competency Five: I can evolve.

To evolve is to grow, flourish, and increase in understanding and wisdom. Nothing stays the same. We can either grow or die. Let the obsolete fade, and welcome the new.

Evolution is a process of cooperation. Where there was previously one working alone, there are now many working in unison. It is the difference between a single cell and a cellular system. Each cell gets more efficient at its job, because the responsibility for survival is now shared. We can become greater than we were before, because we now see what can be accomplished with unity rather than division. At times we get caught in the story or the perceived setback. However, as we grow, these moments pass quickly and at times can even go unnoticed. The evolving attitude desires getting our thinking aligned with what is possible if we cooperate.

As we get older, we settle into the disposition that we have lived. We meet most of the day with a "better-than" mentality. We barely let people finish their sentences before rushing in with, "I know, I know." We have little tolerance for intently listening to another's opinion. We want them to hear ours, agree with ours, and even praise ours. Saying "I know" all the time is a form of arrogance. Not only do we not know everything, we actually know very little relative to all there is to learn. What we are really saying is, "I don't want to hear it again" or "Don't tell me what to do; your opinion doesn't matter."

All that we truly know is that we don't know how to apply much of the information in our head. Just because we know something does not mean we've practiced it. What we've done is commit it to memory so that we can repeat it. But we have little practical experience. Rather than just being clear that we have the words committed to memory, why not take it a step further and see how we can experience that knowledge? We'd rather not. We don't want to be uncomfortable. New experiences are not on the radar unless they are accidental. We don't want to consciously walk into a situation that we can't get out of quickly. We definitely don't want to look foolish. Not only do we remain stagnant in our personal growth, we are dying.

Biology shows that a living thing is either flourishing (growing) or degenerating (dying). As living things, we are subject to these same natural laws. If we are not flourishing, we are degenerating. This is happening through body, mind, and spirit. Our physical body is dying. Our intelligent mind is dying. Our spirit and communication with each other is dying.

We grow physically through nourishment and exercise. We grow intellectually—both consciously and subconsciously—through education and experiences. We grow spiritually through our connection to the field and our higher self. While we may be past the years of physical growth, we can still broaden our knowledge of nutrition and care for our body with exercise. While we have an excellent education, we still do not know everything, nor have we experienced it all. While we may be spiritually grounded in a religious organization or a personal philosophy, there is still room for us to heighten our awareness of humanity. When we deprive ourselves of growth, we sever our connection to life. It is an arduous act to destroy what is our biological imperative. Somehow, though, the agony is familiar, so we do it anyway. Willingness to grow in all areas will be our best chance for embodying our new, victorious, and sober identity.

The very nature of growth implies a degree of pain. It is a bursting forth, a breaking through to something greater. It is freeing when it—whether a seedling or our new awareness—has broken through, but the breaking through can be tormenting. Walk through the redwoods. Imagine for a moment the energy that created thousands of trees that are easily over three hundred feet tall with trunk diameters of ten to twenty feet. Many of these trees will mature in four hundred to five hundred years. We are no less magnificent a species than these beautiful trees. We have no less potential to become this amazing. The question becomes, are we willing?

We are designed to grow and prosper. We often see change as bad, but the universe simply sees it as evolution. While we don't keep our bodies or our minds forever, we can certainly make this life on earth what we choose. The key is to find out if we are willing to grow. If we are not, we are in for rough waters. Life is going to keep happening—with or without our permission. We can either flow with it or get shuffled along. The choice is always ours.

In the end, we learn that when we accept what is happening, the pain of growth no longer seems like pain. Rather, it feels like a soft wind nudging us in a new direction. We have learned that we can change without being in pain. When we resist the wind, we struggle. When we move with the wind, it is effortless. These two propositions are always available to us. One or the other is always prepared to emerge.

There are both our design and the design of those around us. We interact primarily within our own design if we are clear on what it is we desire. We interact primarily on others' designs when we are unclear about what we desire. If we are feeling like we are being pulled into another's agenda, it is because we have allowed ourself to be. We allow ourself to be pulled in because we lack clarity on what we want to be, to do, or to create. We take no action of our own, and then we feel corralled by someone else's plan.

When we agree that we will work on this evolving competency, we are agreeing to take a stand for what we believe to be in our best interest. Before we can take a stand, we need to know our options. We don't lobby against tobacco if we smoke. We don't drink if we want recovery. We get clear on who we are by understanding our personal philosophy. Only when we have distinguished our philosophy can we embody it. Our actions are congruent with our words. Our words are congruent with our actions. We are who we say we are.

When we share a common philosophy with others, our collective consciousness affects all whose lives we touch. Recall the capability of a single cell versus the capability of a cellular system. There is potential in numbers. Not only do we get to grow and blossom, we get to help those around us do the same. We have learned; now we can teach. Our grasp of the interconnected universe will advance. When it advances for us, it advances for everyone. One person can change everything, and that person can be us.

We've known our whole life that we need to continue to grow and prosper. Now we have the opportunity to step out of familiar yet unhealthy patterns and step into something magnificent. Which choice will we make? All paths are hard until they are not. No longer can our fear of change rule us. Our current situation will change, guaranteed, and it may not be for the better. But our isolation and denial leaves us falling further into the abyss, further away from others. It is the decision to change that is so painful, not the actual change itself. Once we have made the decision, the ways and means to achieve will arrive. First we need to decide whether or not we want to change. When this is firm, the balance will follow.

If we find that we are trying, and life *seems* not to be improving, one of two things is happening. We have either not committed to making any real changes, or we have failed to recognize and be grateful for the small changes. We are being impatient and wanting more than our efforts warrant. Life is getting better in some subtle way. Because we lack the ability to see this improvement does not mean it has not occurred. Our true intention and effort does not go unnoticed by the universe. There is no such thing as, *it's not working*. There is only, *we're not allowing it to work*. It is we who have not made the leap. We are the ones who have not severed our ties, not the universe.

The universe is clear and has a perfect balance, an orchestrated rhythm. When we are in alignment with the universal laws, we can watch our lives transform. If we fight the natural order of things, we struggle. The world isn't treating us differently from anyone else; the same rules apply to everyone. What we put out is what we get back. What we reap is what we sow. Until we become utterly willing to change, our life in the future will resemble our life today (or worse than today) for a very long time. Have we had enough? We certainly hope so.

Ninth Challenge: Create a list of competencies that you already possess. Identify where your strengths lie. Create a second list of competencies you wish to sharpen or acquire. These items represent what you are growing toward and will help you determine which action to take.

The purpose of developing these competencies is to see where our values lie. When we see where our values lie, we can better determine what will fulfill us in life. Who do we want to be? We have roles as a spouse, parent, child, friend, family member, work associate, work leader, etc.

The way we behaved today is the person we agreed to be today.

As we identify who we want to be and prepare a statement about who this person is, we are setting in motion our new identity. As we identify and work toward the qualities we wish to possess, we change the trajectory of our life on a daily basis. We go from putting out the fires of our incompetence to preventing fires by preparing for the inevitable storms. Values rooted in principles give us the strongest chance for survival and growth. What have we valued in the past? We've valued secrecy, shame, and delusions. What do we now value? We value truth, integrity, and reality.

As we move forward in this journey, we will learn more about developing our principles and living in accordance and harmony with ourself.

Tenth Challenge: Design a mission statement. A mission statement includes both long—and short-term goals. Within the context of what you ultimately wish to accomplish, you can live each day with this end result in mind. What is it you want to accomplish with your life?

Dialogue 5

December 2004: Sobriety—Day 278

A: *What's up with you today?*

B: *I told my husband the truth. It's so nice to have that off my back. And it wasn't as bad as I thought.*

A: *He might use that against you. Did you ever think of that?*

B: *I did, as a matter of fact. It's okay if he does. I'll deal with that if it happens.*

A: *Don't start telling him the truth about everything. You're not going to start that, are you?*

B: *Are you ever quiet? Can I just have one moment to feel good about myself?*

A: *Just one—don't want you getting too full of yourself.*

B: *I doubt that will happen with you around to criticize me. Anyway, never mind. I'm not going to listen to you now. I'm feeling good.*

Part V: The Partnership

The very word *partner* implies that there is more than one person involved. Whom should we have this partnership with? For those struggling in recovery or those pursuing recovery, this can be a hurdle. Learning to partner with something or someone we can trust seems a near-impossible feat, and lack of a trustworthy partnership keeps many from achieving a recovered life. Not only does this deficiency block recovery, it hinders us from an accomplished, meaningful life. Our very existence has been based on the fact that we could never trust others, and we certainly couldn't trust ourselves. The thought of moving forward and actually trusting ourselves has always seemed impossible. We've let ourselves down so many times. It defies the imagination to think that the next attempt might be any different. Again, we all have a breaking point. Long-term sobriety begins with one day of sobriety. Every recovered alcoholic has had Day One of sobriety, followed by Day Two. We start like everyone else—at Day One.

If we were not raised with any understanding of a source outside of ourself, this notion can be unfathomable. We were programmed to believe that we are alone. The idea of partnership is simple: it involves having a relationship with ourself at more than one level. Helping these levels to communicate harmoniously will be the chief aim of this section.

Knowingly or not, we have been in partnership with one person our whole life—ourself. That indistinct voice within our head that sounds exactly like us has a relationship with us. Although it is voiceless to the outside world, it is constantly speaking, at times even more than we would prefer. It never leaves or goes on vacation. It is there when we dream and when we awaken. It has been a constant companion, whether we like what it says or not. Furthermore, it is never going away.

This partnership we have with ourself is self relating to self. While it appears there is only one person in our head, that one is having a dialogue all day long. When we are awake, we are functioning both subconsciously and consciously. Even when we are asleep, our subconscious mind never rests. It is busy all the time. What is it thinking? Whatever is programmed, whatever is learned, whatever is believed to be true. It has a constant dialogue with us based on our belief system. Our belief system has created our life and will continue to do so, whether or not we are conscious of it.

The question now becomes this: What sort of dialogue do we *want* to have with ourself?

Dividing the self into two separate entities, we have a higher self and a lower self. Here are some generalities showing how each part might see the world. The chart is a basic way to identify what place we are coming from when we hear our head talking. If we aren't sure who is speaking, we can learn to recognize the speaker by his motives.

Lower Self	Higher Self
Self-seeking	Thinks of all, including self
I come first	We are all equal
Competition	Cooperation
Smaller picture/short-term	Larger picture/long-term

Our higher self operates from a place of compassion and acceptance. Motives are rooted in the greatest good. Our lower self operates from self-centeredness and criticism. Motives are rooted in what is best for us—right now!

When we are actively immersed in alcoholism, and even for some time after we stop drinking, we function very much from our lower-self perspective. This is exactly how we can justify our dysfunctional behavior. We think little of others. We take them for granted and expect that they will always put up with our behavior.

As we grow into a new people, we naturally care about all. We are no longer oblivious to what is happening around us. The world looks fundamentally different from within our sober state. This new sober connection with our higher self will be the gateway to our new existence. When we begin to see that we are part of a bigger picture and that all people are created equal, we open up to the abundance of the universe. When we invest in seeing the cause and effect of our actions, we are given a gift. No longer is it okay to take advantage of others or consistently put self first without regard for others. Not because we can't, but because we no longer want to. We value integrity. And when we act against our values, we feel terrible inside.

So here we are, struggling to get sober or maybe just questioning whether we even want sobriety. If we are still undecided, the dialogue will be most heated when the pressure is on. Pressure means that we have just created some chaos for ourself or others and are scheming how to work our way out of it. We have painted ourself into a corner, and now we want to sneak out without anyone seeing our footprints.

Impossible. While we may have done this in the past, there comes a day for us all when we have no more tricks to use. Time's up. It's over. Yet our brain is still rummaging for a great excuse, someone to blame! We all arrive at the day when there is no more justification for our behavior. Yet our mind, so daringly persuasive, will go to any length to convince us that we have one more chance out there. The day we see that we'll never make it while drinking is the best day of the rest of our lives. It admittedly feels like the worst. In truth, it is not.

We have been at war for so long with our addiction that we question how a life without addiction would feel. Not only are we physically addicted, we are also mentally addicted. Our whole identity is associated with a person who has to drink and drug to function. We are at a total loss as to how to relinquish this identity to which we have grown so accustomed. What is the point of it all if we can't enjoy a cocktail every now and then? The problem is that it was never a cocktail; rather it was many cocktails and many problems. The luxury of drinking socially was gone long ago, and somehow this alcohol-filled life seems necessary and sickly normal. This daily drinking or black-out drinking or binge drinking all seems acceptable. It is not, but we have convinced ourself that it is.

Absolutely nothing could be further from the truth, and we, sadly, are the last to see it. When we finally do see it, it's because it has become so glaring that it can no longer be ignored.

If we have fallen into the category of "dry" (no alcohol/no drugs) but have no new thinking and no support in our journey, we find ourself in the same position: a miserable existence that we pretend is okay. Many of us are waiting for the day when we can drink again. We thought alcohol was the problem, but we come to realize that *we* are the problem and alcohol was our pitiful solution. We still are the problem, but now we have no solution. We've cut the damage down by not drinking, but we have not learned how to live effectively with our thinking. We need new tools if we are to succeed. The first tool we will want to cultivate is a relationship with ourself—a *trusting* relationship.

How do we trust ourself after so many years of lying? Trust is something that develops. It does not arrive today in its entirety. It is maturing, unhurriedly and with hard work. Imagine dropping a piece of sand into a bottle each day. It will not look like much at first, but soon it will be a small mound of sand. Over our lifetime, the bottle will fill because we put a grain in every day. This is what it feels like to build trust with ourself. At first, it seems like nothing. As time passes, it begins to appear as something. The sand eventually becomes something substantial, all because we invested our effort a little each day. Begin by doing things a little differently today, not tomorrow.

A simple guide to help us is this: If the typical day goes A-B-C and we no longer want to have B in the routine, we will need to create a new B. We can't just jump to C; our subconscious mind won't let us. It's programmed to follow the routine. The conscious mind isn't strong enough. We can say all the affirmations we want, but the conscious processor isn't strong enough to override the subconscious mind. It won't allow change so easily. Where there was once a B, there is now a void, and the mind will seek to repeat B if we don't allow something new into that space. Most people just decide that they will no longer do B and expect that trying to eliminate or jump over it will be enough. While this may have worked for some people, it is generally not the condition under which we find permanent change occurring. If it was this easy, sobriety would not be an issue to attain. If B is "to have a drink," this is what is programmed to happen. The best chance we have of combating this craving is to remove ourself from that environment. Until our subconscious mind reprograms a new routine, it will seek the old. This will happen without our consent. This is why we stay addicted, even when we don't want to be addicted. This is why we eliminate the offending substance. This is the reason for abstinence.

The guide we had when we drank was our alcohol guide—not the best guide, but the only one we thought we had. If we are new to sobriety, we are moving from an alcohol guide to an unknown guide. Not a very reassuring one, this unknown guide. The key for us will be to identify who or what this new guide is. We already know how to put our belief into something. For years or decades, we've put our belief into drugs or alcohol. Not only did we put our belief into drugs or alcohol, we worshipped them. We revered them. It is okay to admit that they were our number-one priority; they were for every recovered addict. They only have power over us if we put them into our body. Otherwise, it's just some liquid or pills sitting in a bottle. No, they do not talk to us and convince us to drink or take them. This is our mind talking. It is our programmed, subconscious mind trying to repeat patterns of behavior. We need to put our faith into something new, to transfer it somewhere, lest the drug—or alcohol-worship continue. Nature doesn't allow a void. When we take something out, something new will come.

For many, this is the stumbling block and, therefore, the missing link in lasting sobriety. It need not be this way. What we do is shift our focus in what we believe. We used to believe in drinking and would go to any length to make that happen. Now we get to believe in sobriety and its rewards, and we go to any length to make *that* happen. We know how to focus our attention. We know how to get what we want, despite the odds. Yet, somehow, when we try to get sober, we decide we can't believe in anything. Was it so easy to believe in alcohol but impossible to believe in anything else?

It is imperative that we recognize our ability to believe, to put our faith into something new. The issue then becomes whether or not we are willing.

Sometimes we are so scared of the work involved that we cower. We've failed before; we might again. So we quit before we even get started.

If we are new to sobriety or have struggled to stay sober, the question "Can I actually do this?" is foremost in our mind. Even before that question arises, we might find ourself asking, "Do I *have* to get sober? Is that really the only way?" If we have concluded that the answer is *no* or *I hope I don't have to*, we will be unable to compete with the subconscious mind. It is already programmed to continue drinking or to remain abstinent for a short period—followed by more drinking. Our reasons for discontinuing drinking must be compelling and will need to remain compelling if we are to stay sober. This earliest stage is desperation. Is our desperation big enough? Are we finally ready to do something about our problem?

If we have managed to remain sober for a period of time but find ourself discontented or thinking about drinking again, we are in a dangerous place. The addictive mind is seductive and can convince us of just about anything. Be warned: if drinking was a problem before, it will probably still be a problem.

We can find comfort in putting our faith into something new. After all, alcohol failed us many times under many circumstances. It finally became apparent that we needed a new guide.

Our Guide

The *universe's intelligence* became our guide. The more we learned about science, the more we learned about ourself. We were subject to the same order. The universe's intelligence showed us that we are interdependent. The universe seemed to function with a certain set of principles and with a certain balance and harmony. We wanted to be a part of that harmony. We liked the predictability and the balance we saw in nature. It was what we wanted in our life.

When we viewed the universe, we saw an intelligence that was beyond perfect. The calculations were so precise and the knowledge so vast. We liked the big-ness and all-inclusiveness of it. It seemed to know what it was doing. Every year, the leaves fell in the autumn, only to reappear in the spring. *Maybe, just maybe, we could get ourself aligned with this intelligence,* we thought. After all, it certainly seemed better than what we currently had, and we longed for something new.

For us, this "intelligence" was the equivalent of God. We saw it as God manifest in form, a type of order which we could physically see, intellectually comprehend, and spiritually experience. Were we willing to believe in this Source? Were we willing to align ourself with it? Something was there, and it was bigger than us or any person we knew. We appreciated the stability we experienced when we were connected with it. We were the type of person who liked to see to believe. We needed and wanted to see. It wasn't that traditional-God had failed us. It was that we could no longer understand what God felt like. We had altered our mind for so long. It all felt like a blur—especially during early sobriety. But now we felt God clearly when we aligned with the universe.

Universal laws, also known as natural laws, are the universe's principles. They are the axioms on which the universe functions—universal because they apply to life within our known universe and laws because they represent a certain order. While we cannot prove them with a mathematical calculation, we accept them as truths because we see evidence of their validity. *Encyclopedia Britannica* offers this definition: "natural law, in philosophy, a system of right or justice held to be common to all humans and derived from nature rather than rules of society."[1]

These newfound laws made our sober platform more solid. Once we deduced that thoughts, words, and emotions were simply forms of energy, we could align with them for the greatest ability to create. We were actively co-creating our reality through the way we interacted with the universe. We were about to embark on living a principled life, and we weren't even aware of it. We were finally basing our life on natural laws—a stable foundation that applied to all humans, regardless. We were no longer relying on people or material things to bring us happiness. We were now investing in behaviors that would change the direction of our life. If they worked, it was because of us. If they did not work, it was because of us. We were the problem, and we were the solution. We had the question, but we also had the answer.

Universal Laws

These twelve laws have been reprinted with permission from *The Light Shall Set You Free* by Norma J. Milanovich and Shirley D. McCune (1996). The application is my personal translation. It shares how I use these laws in my sober and recovered life.

1. The Law of Divine Oneness

   Application: All creation is interconnected. I may perceive that I am separate, an island, but this is an illusion. Despite my previous thinking, my actions matter to me and all those around me. I can no longer pretend I am only hurting myself when I drink. I can no longer pretend I know how to think reasonably in the absence of spiritual awareness. My actions and my thoughts about my actions affect the energy around me. My isolated and self-serving attitude will be transformed if, a) I am willing to stay sober, and b) I am willing to work on growing spiritually.

2. The Law of Vibration

   Application: All things seen and unseen, when broken down to their smallest form are energy. This energy has a frequency, a vibration. Energy can only be converted from one form to another. It can never be created or destroyed. My spoken word, quiet thought, and physical action transmit vibration. This vibration is cyclical. What I think matters. I can learn to discipline my thinking. My lack of discipline and loving thinking is perpetuating a situation I say I do not want. The potential energy is there for me to make a change. I am not a victim. I have freewill.

3. The Law of Action

   Application: If I want something new I get to be willing to do something new. It is through action that I manifest the quality of my life. Everything I now possess is the product of how I think, express, feel and act. Only *my* action will produce the desired result. If I am waiting for another to make a decision for my life to be better I am mistaken. This is not happening . . . ever! If I want to stop drinking I get to be willing to go to any length to stop drinking. If I want new thinking I get to go to any length to get new thinking. It all requires action.

4. The Law of Correspondence

   Application: What is happening in the material (seen) world is also happening in the non-material (unseen) world. Nothing is happening outside of me that I have not already welcomed or allowed on the inside of me. My body, mind, and spirit are intertwined. If I struggle with recovery from alcoholism I must see that I struggle in all areas. I struggle with physical craving, lack of mental clarity, and spiritual awareness.

5. The Law of Cause and Effect

   Application: For every action there is a corresponding reaction. I cannot do anything I want and expect to feel good about myself. I get to do loving action that is in alignment with my principles. This is when I feel best. If I don't like how I am feeling I take a look at what I did or did not do to cause me to feel this way. The universe always gives me what I need. And, there is always a blessing if I am willing to see it. I experience pain when I am not willing to see the best in any given situation. Just because I am uncomfortable does not mean I get to drink, yell, hit, rage or run. I get to face my feelings and see how the situation serves me.

6. The Law of Compensation

   Application: Financial or material blessings are the physical manifestation of my actions. If I want to get more out of life then I must give more. Not give more to get more, but give more because I like the way it feels. I like who I am being when I am giving. As a recovered alcoholic I get to help and support others in need. I need not always be thinking of myself. I can expect to receive, in proportion, to the measure that I give . . . unconditionally!

7. The Law of Attraction

Application: Like attracts like. I'll get back what I put out. Be mindful of my words and thoughts, they precede my actions either consciously or subconsciously. I get back what I have given. The normal challenges of early sobriety are just those . . . normal challenges. I attract newness to my life by acting new. I must first get myself in alignment with who I want to be—today. Then I must be willing to be that person—today. It is then that the universe responds in like.

8. The Law of Perpetual Transmutation of Energy

Application: I have all I need to become someone new. Applying learned information to my actions is what changes my life. Higher vibration transforms lower vibration. When I surround myself with recovered addicts I increase my positive energy. When I support another addict to recover I increase in positive energy. As I grow, I have a responsibility to help another and thus raise the consciousness of the planet. My recovery matters to humanity. When one heals we all heal.

9. The Law of Relativity

Application: We all experience our own set of situations in life. No one is exempt from these rites of passage. These situations have the power to initiate growth or welcome decay. One of the two will always happen. All things are relative. My alcoholism is my situation to grow through. There are always two distinct ways to see a situation. If I want sobriety I will get good at seeing situations from an unbiased perspective. Remembering that life could always be worse than it is. Be grateful. If I think a month of sobriety is no big deal, I can go ahead and drink and then try to get that month once more. It won't be easy. The first few days will seem like hell (again).

10. The Law of Polarity

Application: Everything has an opposite. Otherwise it would not exist in our world. There is no *up* without a *down*, no *here* without a *there*. Because I see only one side does not mean the reverse is nonexistent. If I want the opposite of what I have, I need to focus my energy on its opposite. Until now, I have only wanted the easy part of life, never the uncomfortable part. Realizing that life comes equal is important to my sobriety. I must be willing to accept the small discomforts that life presents. I must be willing to accept them with an unaltered frame of mind.

11. The Law of Rhythm

Application: All things vibrate with a rhythm. The seasons arrive on time in a certain cycle. Sadness is never experienced without having known joy. Death is not preceded by birth. There is a certainty to the way that life moves forward. I learn to function within this natural rhythm. Just because I am sober does not mean that only the good in life is coming. Sobriety does not wipe out the possibility for issues to arise. What I learn is that I can handle life, unaltered, as life comes toward me. Negative things will happen, and I can choose to rise above them. A fulfilled and happy life is not free of challenges. Don't get stuck in a nonproductive rhythm. It will perpetuate itself. I accept the day as it unfolds because I know that my best thinking and planning was implemented. Beyond this I have learned I am not in charge.

12. The Law of Gender

Application: I possess energy that is both masculine and feminine. The balance of these two is what creates harmony in my life. When one is out of balance, both are out of balance. My feminine is creative, compassionate, and concerned. My masculine is logical, analytical and driven. When I express all these attributes from a place of strength and love I create the optimum environment to flourish. I need not be one way. There is dimension to my person. As a sober person I can embrace my past and love myself fully. I grow into all of me. That was who I was yesterday. This is who I am today. *This is who I am becoming.*

Implementing the laws brings strength to both the structure and foundation of our recovery. We will no longer need someone to tell us the difference between right and wrong. We no longer need to wait and hope no one noticed our behavior. We no longer need to worry about what we did the night before or who we have to apologize to the next day. We are free. We no longer behave out of the desire to avoid a bad consequence. We genuinely desire to reap the rewards of feeling good about ourself, who we are and who we are becoming.

If we are new to sobriety, we will experience distress. This painful confrontation is an inevitable and unavoidable rite of passage. If we are fortunate enough to land in a twelve-step meeting, better yet. Take advantage of the wisdom and recovery. It will be a chance to acquire friends who travel a similar path and who help each other. As we begin to cultivate a new dialogue with ourself, we will become clear on when the lower self is speaking and when the higher self is speaking. What was once acceptable behavior will no longer be tolerated. While this change may appear slow and immeasurable, we do not despair. If we keep focused on our principles, we will prevail.

What often happens is that the result doesn't come soon enough, so we abandon the project. Remembering the key competencies will move us through anything. The dialogue with ourselves is the hardest part. We will be continuously required to hold ourself accountable to our higher self. This is easier to do when we are working with a life coach or a mentor. Once we are out of their earshot, however, we are left to our own devices. Our thinking will drag us down in a heartbeat if we aren't clear on what we want. We need to give ourselves time to grow into being accountable to ourselves, with ourselves. We must get clear on what we want. Even if we're scared, it's okay. We all are. And as we develop accountability with our higher self, we will begin to see that the partnership has extended beyond ourselves to those we trust. We will succeed.

The next natural step for us to achieve is the trust of those around us. As others become aware of the change in us, they will be more willing to let us back into their world again. This in turn fuels our feelings of love for ourselves. We are finally recovering. We are experiencing our own trustworthiness. This is one of the rewards of sobriety. We get to like and love ourself again, and so do those around us. What was initially a new relationship growing within has now grown to include those we love.

We cannot expect perfection when we are moving through these challenges. One of the greatest gifts we can give ourself is time. It took time to get where we are; it will take time to get things turned around. We believe that the principles are working for us, because they are. If we aren't getting what we want, we take a closer look at what we are putting out. Observation is the key to change. If we don't see something, we can't change it. If we feel good about our part, then we get the lesson of patience. Things don't always happen in our time or the way we think they should.

The light only seems more radiant because it has been dark. The light has always been there. Everything is balanced and equal, always. If we think we are receiving worse than we gave, we are mistaken. If we think we are getting more than we deserve, we are mistaken. The universe is balanced. If we perceive that it is imbalanced, it is because we have not yet mastered the competency of reframing.

We no longer think that terrible things are happening. We just realize that life is happening and everything has a purpose. Just because we do not see the purpose at this moment doesn't mean it's not there. It simply means we cannot see it. Truth just *is*. Our believing it or not does not change it.

We all know that feeling we get, maybe months or years after something terrible had happened, when we finally understand why it happened. That's the feeling we're talking about: the understanding that it all makes sense and that it had to happen the way it happened. Then we become almost thankful for the experience. This is the universe doing for us and creating on our behalf. Learning to recognize that this is always happening is a gift beyond measure.

At this juncture, some of us may be resisting the idea of the universe and the laws it possesses. This is not a problem. Let them reveal themselves. We ask the universe to show us, and it will. A universal law will often show itself as a crazy coincidence. Sometimes we like it; sometimes we do not. Either way, we are learning the truth of what is.

Einstein said, "A man should look for what is, and not for what he thinks should be."[2] For addicts, this is the secret of life. We've spent years looking for the way we thought things should be. It never occurred to us to look for what is. There is so much joy in what is happening now. The challenge is to learn how to see it. When we stop resisting, we are finally free.

This concept always seemed backward in our minds. Freedom supposedly came from our detachment, not from our connection. Now the universe is teaching us that our freedom comes from our connection. We are designed to be interdependent. There is balance in our interdependence. Connecting with the Source within, our higher self, will be the connection that not only saves our life but allows it to flourish. We no longer need to be afraid to listen to the self-dialogue in our heads when we are making decisions. We will hear clearly who is speaking. If by chance we cannot tell or have not honed that skill yet, we will—with time and practice. Until then, see that we are connected to other resources. If our circle of influence is a healthy one, a means will appear that will help guide us. We ask, and then we become aware when the help manifests.

This can be a difficult place, the waiting place. Our old identity said we needed it when we needed it. Our new identity understands that it arrives when it arrives. Many times we do not get the things we request, because we are not ready to receive them or because it is not in our best interest to receive them at this time. We are never being punished or tested, even though it can feel this way. The universe knows that our request is not yet in alignment with what we are capable of understanding.

We plant bulbs in the dead of winter only to wait for their blossom in spring. Their environment—soil, water, and sun—will see that they flourish. The same is true for us. We think we should be blossoming when it is only time to be planted. We want to blossom, but it is only time for the seed to open. We really want to blossom, yet we barely grow roots. We believe strongly that it is time to blossom as we absorb nourishment from the soil. We are growing stronger. Still, we can't believe we aren't blossoming, yet we are only ready to break the surface of the soil. This is absolutely taking too much time. We cannot see that our roots are growing deeper, our stem thicker. When will the day come when we will blossom? We should have been there already; we are sure of it. Can't the universe see how hard we have been trying? Why won't it let us blossom? All the while, the bud is tightly sealed. *Why?* we ask. *Why aren't things changing? Why aren't we blossoming? What have we done wrong?*

The day finally arrives when the bud opens to the magnificence of the sun's light. It is finally blossoming. All these moments, all these days and weeks and months, we were preparing to blossom. We just couldn't see it.

Many moments lie between wanting and receiving. They are necessary and invaluable. Notice what is changing. Observe the ways we are getting stronger. Know that what is next is what is supposed to come next. There is order to the universe. We are part of that order. Stop resisting that order. When the ovum and sperm fuse, they will divide and multiply thousands of times before they even slightly resemble a human. One cell will grow to billions, each cell expressing itself differently. Some cells will form organs, while others form bone. And yet with all our technology, we still do not know how each cell knows what to become.

These same phenomena are at work in our lives. What we do know is that, in roughly nine months, we will have a new life. There is an "intelligence," an order in the process. The fetus will not be mature in a month or two, no matter how much we anticipate its arrival. It is coming when it is coming and not a moment sooner. The same is true for us now. Resistance will only delay the fertilization, not the inevitable. What is the evitable? If we are an alcoholic, we will always be an alcoholic. No amount of denial will change this fact. Denial will only delay the solution.

When we resist the order of things, we are, in effect, saying that we know best how things should be. Is this true? Do we know best? When we look at the whole of our life, how well have we been running the show? For most of us, the answer is *not very*. Rather than proceed with the old thinking, maybe we can try to move forward with new thinking. It was Socrates who said, "The only true wisdom is in knowing you know nothing."[3] We do not know everything. Maybe we can slow down or even stop trying to figure it all out. Maybe we can just stay focused on us and what we are creating in our life.

As we awaken this partnership within, we will be opening ourself up for everything to appear. To paraphrase a portion of a 1992 lecture in Santa Monica, California, by Marianne Williamson: *When I invited God into my life, I thought he was going to come in and make everything beautiful. He didn't. He showed up with a wrecking ball and said we needed to start over, from the foundation up.*

If our life has felt this way, we are in the company of every recovered addict. It is the modest beginning of something extraordinary. We just can't see it yet! The old will need to be shattered before we can start new. The cracking, breaking, falling, and inevitable crashing of the old identity torments us. It becomes our initiation. It happened that way because that's what it took for us to see it.

Over time, we learn that not much is unbearable. Even the actual experience of agony, in hindsight, is not as horrible as we might have imagined it would be. We often marvel at the fact that we walked through it. We even tell others it wasn't so bad. Life appears to be a peculiar set of fortuity. We are usually so afraid of new experiences that we neglect to acknowledge them, and rarely do we enjoy them. Yet often when they come to pass, we express gratitude for having had the opportunity. How refreshing it is to know that we can adopt this perspective at any moment. We needn't wait until the end. Adopting this new attitude may sound like this: *Universe, show us how we can achieve this if this is what we are to achieve. Universe, help us to not question the order of things; and, Universe, open us to experiences that allow us to grow into our greater self.*

Be attentive. Just because we are asking for help does not mean it will arrive the way we want it to. It will, however, arrive.

When we open up and get aligned with the way things are, another peculiar thing happens. Much of what we *don't* want seems to also appear, as if to throw us off track. At times it can almost feel like a force that does not want our success. It is not. It just feels that way. We are taking an old identity that wants to hang on and replacing it with a new identity that has yet to take root. Being clear on our decision will allow us to maneuver through these moments with more ease—not easily, but rather with greater ease than if we had we not been clear about our decision. When we are undecided, we quickly get pulled back in by the subconscious mind—so quickly that we cannot even explain what has happened. With every fiber of our being, we cannot explain our behavior. We are at a total loss.

The familiar situation for alcoholics is that we have allowed ourselves to drink again. We are as perplexed as anyone. But it is no enigma. The drink was the result of not living life the way we could be living it. We let the gifts of integrity, trust, and partnership slip away. We quit having compassion. We judged. We forgot what it was to forgive. We stopped telling the truth. We shirked responsibilities. We lacked courage. We forgot what it meant to remain dedicated and disciplined. We were ungrateful. We ultimately stopped trusting ourself. It wasn't long before a drink seemed like a good idea. The lower self was swift to detect our lost connection. It quickly and ever-so-gently assured us that it was okay, even necessary, to drink.

If we are to be released from the seduction of alcohol, we must prepare. Expect a battle; it is coming. Our mind is not ready to release its old beliefs, at least not without a struggle. The discomfort and the agony are part of the process. Stop thinking it should be easy. Stop thinking it should be effortless. It will require our best efforts. Now is the time to stay connected with our higher self. Now is the time to cultivate a relationship, a partnership with a Source and resources we can trust. Now is the time to stay connected to our principles. Unwavering and unchanging, they will carry us through. That is a guarantee.

Dialogue 6

A: *Well, I guess you made it. Good job. You can drink now. You made it past your one-year mark.*

B: *I don't want to drink today.*

A: *Are you serious? This was the agreement! One year.*

B: *I know. I've changed my mind. Maybe tomorrow. I just don't want to drink today. You can ask me again tomorrow. Anyhow, I'm busy. Look at the beautiful pictures the kids made. I love them sooooooo much. I'm so lucky to have them.*

..

Part VI: The Basics

The basics are the work, the hard work we do to actually attain and sustain a sober identity. If we want to be good at anything, we practice. Athletes are strong and skilled because they master their minds and their bodies respond. They are not different from us. If we want to succeed, we need to master our minds and our bodies will follow.

The body does nothing that the mind does not tell it to do. The body houses the blueprint; the mind tells it what to do and how to build. If we want success, we plan for it. We do this preparation through our thoughts, and more importantly, through our actions. We act in accordance with our principles. Our principles are the standards we choose to live by. We decide who we want to be and set out to become that person: we do the chore even when we are tired; we journal though we'd rather not write; we read rather than watch television; we say "Hello" even when we feel lonely (*especially* when we are feeling lonely); we recognize that others are in need, even when we perceive that we are the needy; and we recognize that there is something to be gained, even when it appears there is not.

When we have spent some time with our mind and have observed how it works, we will be capable of changing our behaviors. The very first thing we must do is observe ourself as honestly as possible. The truth of ourself will reveal itself. From there we can decide when (or if) we want to change that behavior. We will spend a great deal of time observing, until we are certain of what we are seeing. There is no room for long-term denial in any area of life.

We must witness ourself from the inside out. Everything comes from within us. Are we willing to take a look? We must not be afraid of the dark spots. They are like the fireworks on the Fourth of July. The colors would never look so magnificent if not for the darkness they illuminate. The darkness lets us see the light with brilliance and beauty. We needn't wish the darkness away. Simply let it be. It will go away on its own, fade away when it is no longer needed. Will it return again? Yes, it will return. This is what it means to be human. When it does, know that it is there to be the backdrop for a new illumination. Everything serves a purpose. When we stop fighting, stop being at war with everything, we can actually begin to enjoy our life.

While observation and awareness will be the initial task, abstinence from alcohol, drugs, and other mind-altering substances is also a necessity. Seek professional counsel on appropriate measures for detoxification from alcohol and drugs. There are many hazards to self-detox, and some can be fatal. We must not let our mind convince us that we know what to do because we've done it before. We can be assured that we do *not* know, with certainty, how to proceed. If we value our life, we will get help.

From detox, we have other options available. These include but are not limited to:

Inpatient or Outpatient Hospital Program

This is a recovery program available through a hospital. Recovery programs begin after detox. Generally, we will detox at the hospital and begin a program immediately. Inpatient care requires us to reside at the facility. Outpatient care allows us to come and go from the facility. These programs are generally thirty to ninety days in duration. An education in addiction and the opportunity to work with a medical doctor are both available at these facilities. This is an excellent opportunity. Seize it if it is made available.

A Recovery Facility/Treatment Center

This is a recovery program that is independent from a hospital. Most offer detox. Check to see which include on-site medical detox, if this is what is needed. Treatment centers are similar to hospital programs in that there is a great deal of education as well as medical treatment. Additionally, they provide individual and group therapy. This is a structured environment. Program length varies, depending on the needs of the patient.

Sober Living Home

This is also a recovery program. We live in a home with other recovering addicts. Homes provide different opportunities. A sober living home can benefit someone who requires the transition back into society or family life. It is similar to a regular home in that all the daily chores need to be taken care of: grocery shopping, laundry, housecleaning, etc. Additionally, these homes provide structure through a planned schedule of events. Events include meetings, groups, workshops, and classes. The goal of the recovery home is to transition the addict back to interdependent living. We can live at a sober living home for a brief or an extended period of time.

Twelve-Step Program

Probably the most familiar of trusted sources is this program. It has morphed from a recovery option for alcoholics to a recovery option for just about any addiction one can imagine. Globally, it is the largest organization serving alcoholics. Newcomers (less than thirty days of sobriety) are encouraged to attend a meeting daily for the first ninety days and to get a sponsor. A sponsor walks us through the steps.

Recovery Coach and Life Coach

If we are new to sobriety, a coach can assist with getting us on a fast and intense track. This is an option for those serious about recovery. Look for a coach who is familiar with addiction or has recovered from addiction. This is not therapy. It is achievement driven. The focus is on today, where we are going, and what we are willing to do to get there. We work with goals, intentions, principles, obstacles, and limiting beliefs. Coaches are action-oriented. A qualified coach will encourage us to take action and hold us accountable.

Being under the care of a medical doctor is encouraged. Doctors with knowledge of addiction are those we should seek. The purpose of a medical doctor is twofold. First, we will want to address any medical issues that have occurred as a consequence of our drinking. Secondly, we will seek help with other issues that may exist (i.e. bipolar, depression, anxiety, dual diagnosis). Oftentimes, these conditions become more prominent when we stop drinking. Take advantage of what is offered and can be afforded. Cutting corners may build an unstable foundation. We can build, but it is prudent to build on level concrete rather than sand. Sand represents the familiar, subconscious mind. The concrete represents the higher self. While this poses possible discomfort, proceed anyway. As long as we are being honest, we will be making movement and achieving. We must get clear on our motive. Omitting information to a health care practitioner is dishonest. Be earnest and straightforward. These will bring the greatest results.

Group workshops, twelve-step groups, and online support groups are invaluable. They will facilitate learning at many levels. Even when we don't particularly enjoy a group, we can gain from observing those in the group. We are not talking about criticism of another. We are talking about noticing how we are judging others. The important thing is that we don't stop trying to connect. We keep looking. We will find an environment that suites us. The seed will not produce the tree if it is left in a jar.

We must keep asking for guidance in the form of direction and clarity. If we find we are not able to make a decision, we probably haven't acquired enough data to make the decision. We ask for the information and never stop asking. Asking opens us up to the possibility that we do not know something. Nature doesn't like a void. The space will be filled. Not asking means we already think we know. The universe cannot do much with this space. It will, however, send us signs. Those signs usually show up in the form of a challenge, an issue, an irritation, or a problem.

This is the universe speaking to us. It is not punishment. It is not unfairness. It is this thing we call *life*. It is always happening and will continue to happen. We needn't agree that it is acceptable. We need only to get in alignment with what is.

While we have never seen the dark side of the moon, we know it is there. We must align ourself with this truth: there is something there, and we cannot see it, but it is there nonetheless. We stay determined at finding the truth of ourself and being honest about what we find. We question all our beliefs to find out if they work for us, keep the ones that do, and let go of the ones that do not. We are willing to see life differently and endure some discomfort as we move through this process.

These are the moments in which we advance. We will evolve into a person who loves himself, a feeling that could never come from a drink—or a thousand drinks. It is permanent, unwavering, and unchangeable. It is sober, and it is the truest freedom we have ever known.

Tools for Change

If we are preparing to make some major life changes, we will want the best support we can find. We want to set ourself up for success rather than failure. How is this accomplished? It starts with a desire, becomes a decision, transitions to a dedication, and finally becomes destiny. There is no other way to get where we say we want to go. If we do the work, it will get done. The universe does not hand us a perfect and polished life simply because we have asked for it. It hands us the tools to obtain a life worth living.

Journaling is an extremely effective method for uncovering deeply rooted feelings, beliefs, and agreements. There is more than one way to journal.

Straight journaling is simply taking a pen to a notebook and writing whatever comes to mind. These entries can be completed in a certain time frame, e.g., ten minutes per day, or by writing until exhaustion. Writing to exhaustion requires the writer to journal until they have unleashed all thought on the subject at hand. This can take ten minutes, but generally it will involve writing for an extended period of time. The goal is to write until we can write no more.

Voice A/Voice B journaling is a method of journaling that was used in the dialogues of this book. "A" represents lower self, the entity that is questioning, and "B" represents higher self, the entity that gives unconditional love. As we evolve spiritually, we will notice that voice "A" gets softer and more loving. This is a clear indicator that we are growing. The dialogue from "A" will be less confrontational over time as we work the Ten Challenges, Five Key Competencies, and study the universal laws. If there is a particularly challenging event or trauma, expect "A" to revert to its old language. This is a normal part of being human. Continue to become aware, observe, and journal. We will notice that we recover from these moments more quickly as time passes.

Letter-to-Source journaling is a method of writing that is similar to A/B. The Letter to Source involves asking Source one or more questions. Once the request is made and the writer is ready to receive his reply from Source, the writer resumes writing. In some instances, the reply is immediate. In others, it can take days or weeks. This method is particularly effective when journaling to God or a person who has passed on. While the writer makes the actual reply letter, he is encouraged to respond with the words and syntax that Source would use, not his own.

Free-form journaling is a method of writing that is not limited in any way. It can include photos, drawings, or memorabilia. It is the freest expression of self in any form the writer may choose.

Much of the work we do in recovery involves writing. If we struggle, we keep practicing. We start with a minimum of one minute per day of free-form journaling. Once we get started, we often find that it is not so easy to stop. We keep adding minutes to our writing time. We can use a timer if our time is limited. This will allow us to stay on task for the remainder of our day while holding us accountable for the minimum of journaling. If we have difficulty writing the old-fashioned way (pen and paper), we can use our computer. Most recovered addicts have spent many, many hours unlocking beliefs. More often than not, this will involve writing. Just write. Regardless of how we feel about it now, we will soon reap the benefits.

The Ten Challenges

Begin today to journal on the ten challenges presented within this book. These journal entries will show you where you are at today, your Point O (point of origin). When you understand your origin, you can effectively move toward your Point D (point of destination).

First Challenge: Start observing your behavior. Become aware of something new about yourself daily.

Second Challenge: Discover whether or not you actually want what it is you say you want. Are your actions in alignment with your desire? If not, what kind of changes are you prepared to make? Journal as much detail as possible. Do not cut corners, and above all else, do not give in to hopelessness. Have faith that this process can work for you.

Third Challenge: Make a list of limiting beliefs that you are aware you have. If you are drawing a blank, these tag words may help: a negative mantra you repeat; prejudices for people, places, or institutions; strong opinions regarding sex, money, education, government, or religion. Add to this list as awareness increases. Once you have identified a belief, notice how that belief affects your behavior. Next, identify what could happen if you stopped behaving according to those thoughts. Journal your answers.

Fourth Challenge: Start to notice when you get what you need rather than what (you think) you want. Recognize the gift that arrived at this moment. Feel and express gratitude that it happened the way it did. Journal your findings.

Fifth Challenge: Notice and list standards that are currently in place in your life. Which of these standards is beneath who you thought you would become? Why has it become acceptable to live this way? Journal about each standard.

Sixth Challenge: Learn what motivates you. Begin identifying patterns that are repetitive. If you are struggling, look back at early childhood achievements and work forward. See if a pattern appears. Journal about achievements that came to fruition as well as those that did not. Both will be revealing.

Seventh Challenge: Become familiar with the feeling of actually stepping through your fears. Journal about what you thought it would feel like versus how it actually felt.

Eighth Challenge: Notice what you are sending out with your silent thoughts. Notice what comes back. Try to spend some time digging and seeing some root beliefs that are positive about you. Focus on those for one day. Notice how you feel at the end of that day.

Ninth Challenge: Create a list of competencies that you already possess. Identify where your strengths lie. Create a second list of competencies you wish to sharpen or acquire. These items represent what you are growing toward and will help you determine which actions to take.

Tenth Challenge: Design a mission statement. A mission statement includes both long—and short-term goals. Within the context of what you ultimately wish to accomplish, you can live each day with this end result in mind. What is it you want to accomplish with your life?

The Five Key Competencies

Begin to apply the key competencies to your daily life. Notice within the competencies that you have natural areas of strength and weakness. Seek balance within all the competencies.

Competency One: I am determined.

We are given the gift of choice. Begin to use it. We are not a victim of alcoholism.

Competency Two: I am straightforward.

Being straightforward is about honesty. Stop hiding from the truth. It will pursue us relentlessly.

Competency Three: I can be navigated.

Navigation is about guidance. We are willing to trust in a new source. We are willing to learn how that source feels.

Competency Four: I can reframe my perspective.

Reframing has two parts. We reframe to see the situation from a new angle. We reframe to grant pardon and experience forgiveness.

Competency Five: I can evolve.

To evolve is to grow, flourish, and increase in understanding and wisdom. Nothing stays the same. We can either grow or die. Let the obsolete fade, and welcome the new.

Universal Laws

Study the universal laws in more depth. Below is my interpretation of the laws. There is more than one version of universal laws as well as sub-laws. See how these principles can be applied to your life.

1. The Law of Divine Oneness

Application: All creation is interconnected. I may perceive that I am separate, an island, but this is an illusion. Despite my previous thinking, my actions matter to me and all those around me. I can no longer pretend I am only hurting myself when I drink. I can no longer pretend I know how to think reasonably in the absence of spiritual awareness. My actions and my thoughts about my actions affect the energy around me. My isolated and self-serving attitude will be transformed if, a) I am willing to stay sober, and b) I am willing to work on growing spiritually.

2. The Law of Vibration

Application: All things seen and unseen, when broken down to their smallest form are energy. This energy has a frequency, a vibration. Energy can only be converted from one form to another. It can never be created or destroyed. My spoken word, quiet thought, and physical action transmit vibration. This vibration is cyclical. What I think matters. I can learn to discipline my thinking. My lack of discipline and loving thinking is perpetuating a situation I say I do not want. The potential energy is there for me to make a change. I am not a victim. I have freewill.

3. The Law of Action

Application: If I want something new I get to be willing to do something new. It is through action that I manifest the quality of my life. Everything I now possess is the product of how I think, express, feel and act. Only *my* action will produce the desired result. If I am waiting for another to make a decision for my life to be better I am mistaken. This is not happening . . . ever! If I want to stop drinking I get to be willing to go to any length to stop drinking. If I want new thinking I get to go to any length to get new thinking. It all requires action.

4. The Law of Correspondence

Application: What is happening in the material (seen) world is also happening in the non-material (unseen) world. Nothing is happening outside of me that I have not already welcomed or allowed on the inside of me. My body, mind, and spirit are intertwined. If I struggle with recovery from alcoholism I must see that I struggle in all areas. I struggle with physical craving, lack of mental clarity, and spiritual awareness.

5. The Law of Cause and Effect

Application: For every action there is a corresponding reaction. I cannot do anything I want and expect to feel good about myself. I get to do loving action that is in alignment with my principles. This is when I feel best. If I don't like how I am feeling I take a look at what I did or did not do to cause me to feel this way. The universe always gives me what I need. And, there is always a blessing if I am willing to see it. I experience pain when I am not willing to see the best in any given situation. Just because I am uncomfortable does not mean I get to drink, yell, hit, rage or run. I get to face my feelings and see how the situation serves me.

6. The Law of Compensation

Application: Financial or material blessings are the physical manifestation of my actions. If I want to get more out of life then I must give more. Not give more to get more, but give more because I like the way it feels. I like who I am being when I am giving. As a recovered alcoholic I get to help and support others in need. I need not always be thinking of myself. I can expect to receive, in proportion, to the measure that I give . . . unconditionally!

7. The Law of Attraction

Application: Like attracts like. I'll get back what I put out. Be mindful of my words and thoughts, they precede my actions either consciously or subconsciously. I get back what I have given. The normal challenges of early sobriety are just those . . . normal challenges. I attract newness to my life by acting new. I must first get myself in alignment with who I want to be—today. Then I must be willing to be that person—today. It is then that the universe responds in like.

8. The Law of Perpetual Transmutation of Energy

Application: I have all I need to become someone new. Applying learned information to my actions is what changes my life. Higher vibration transforms lower vibration. When I surround myself with recovered addicts I increase my positive energy. When I support another addict to recover I increase in positive energy. As I grow, I have a responsibility to help another and thus raise the consciousness of the planet. My recovery matters to humanity. When one heals we all heal.

9. The Law of Relativity

Application: We all experience our own set of situations in life. No one is exempt from these rites of passage. These situations have the power to initiate growth or welcome decay. One of the two will always happen. All things are relative. My alcoholism is my situation to grow through. There are always two distinct ways to see a situation. If I want sobriety I will get good at seeing situations from an unbiased perspective. Remembering that life could always be worse than it is. Be grateful. If I think a month of sobriety is no big deal, I can go ahead and drink and then try to get that month once more. It won't be easy. The first few days will seem like hell (again).

10. The Law of Polarity

Application: Everything has an opposite. Otherwise it would not exist in our world. There is no *up* without a *down*, no *here* without a *there*. Because I see only one side does not mean the reverse is nonexistent. If I want the opposite of what I have, I need to focus my energy on its opposite. Until now, I have only wanted the easy part of life, never the uncomfortable part. Realizing that life comes equal is important to my sobriety. I must be willing to accept the small discomforts that life presents. I must be willing to accept them with an unaltered frame of mind.

11. The Law of Rhythm

Application: All things vibrate with a rhythm. The seasons arrive on time in a certain cycle. Sadness is never experienced without having known joy. Death is not preceded by birth. There is a certainty to the way that life moves forward. I learn to function within this natural rhythm. Just because I am sober does not mean that only the good in life is coming. Sobriety does not wipe out the possibility for issues to arise. What I learn is that I can handle life, unaltered, as life comes toward me. Negative things will happen, and I can choose to rise above them. A fulfilled and happy life is not free of challenges. Don't get stuck in a nonproductive rhythm. It will perpetuate itself. I accept the day as it unfolds because I know that my best thinking and planning was implemented. Beyond this I have learned I am not in charge.

12. The Law of Gender

Application: I possess energy that is both masculine and feminine. The balance of these two is what creates harmony in my life. When one is out of balance, both are out of balance. My feminine is creative, compassionate, and concerned. My masculine is logical, analytical and driven. When I express all these attributes from a place of strength and love I create the optimum environment to flourish. I need not be one way. There is dimension to my person. As a sober person I can embrace my past and love myself fully. I grow into all of me. That was who I was yesterday. This is who I am today. *This is who I am becoming.*

Quick-Reference Guide for Shifting Our Thinking

Refer to this quick-reference guide to discipline your mind and shift its thinking. The following are examples of how to reframe and replace unloving thoughts with loving thoughts:

Unloving	Loving
I need to.	I get to.
I want more.	Thank you.
I can't.	I can.
I want it now.	I can wait.
This is happening *to* me.	This is happening *for* me.
This isn't what I expected.	This is what I can bring.
I quit.	I can proceed despite discomfort.
This can't be happening to me.	This is the way it is.
This is impossible.	The reward is worth the effort.
I can trust no one.	I can trust.
There are too many obstacles.	This exists for me to walk through it.
Things are not going the way I want, and it's not my fault.	Things are not going the way I wished; I will be loving anyway.
They treat me so poorly.	No one treats me worse than I've treated myself.
I hate when things change.	I can adapt.
My hands are tied.	I have a choice.
I don't see it; it must not be there.	It exists because I see evidence of it.
I'll let them know what I really think.	There are so many things I do not need to say today.
I don't know how, and I'll never learn how.	I have the capability and the willingness.

You need to do this for me.	If I do not do it, it will go un-done.
I must hang on.	I can let go.
My feelings are the enemy.	My feelings are the gift.
I'll pull it off.	There are always natural consequences.
You always make me feel bad.	My mind-set determines my day.
I hate feeling this.	Why am I feeling this?
I hate when things get in my way.	I understand what it means to persevere.
I can't stand being around those people.	My adversaries are among my greatest teachers.
I wish they liked me.	I'm powerless over what others think of me.
Somebody's going to pay for this.	I can manage this problem.
I need to run.	Courage means I stay despite my fear.
I'll pretend it's okay.	This is no longer my choice.
Nothing matters.	Moments matter.
What can I get?	What can I give?
I do things my way.	I can do things someone else's way.
I don't need others.	I can ask for help.
I'm wasting my time.	It's worth the effort.
I have to.	I'm willing.
I need.	I have enough.

For most of my life, everything was about being seen on the top of the mountain. It is no longer about being seen, nor is it about being on top. It's about all the little things I do every day to keep climbing. I enjoy that I get to climb. I enjoy reaching the peak because I have been willing to persevere. The journey is the magnificence, not because anyone notices, but because *I* notice. It is not so much the gold medal as it is all the moments I practiced—even when I didn't feel like it. It's about all those moments when I never gave up. I receive a reward that is unmatched: a whole and complete me.

No longer is my existence focused on drinking or not drinking. I am freed from that nagging idea. My life has now become so much more. To drink or not to drink has a shallowness that I had previously never seen. Could this have been the greatest question in my life, professing my right to drink? Was this the depth of my person? It seems shocking to look back and recognize the lives I endangered and the consequences I and others endured. It would seem ugly, my glaring lack of character, were it not for its obvious beauty. I am awestruck to see the synergy of so much that previously went unrecognized. I almost missed out on my life, and I didn't even know it. I am fortunate. So are you, if you are reading these words. Your life has far more substance than you are aware of. It is all there waiting for you to recall it. It has always been there.

The first thought always just appears as if out of nowhere. The appearance of the thought is not the problem; but what I do with the thought is the answer. I always have the choice to act on it or release it and ask for something new. If I like my first thought, then my second thought will be the plan for manifesting it. This is followed by action. If I do not like my first thought, I can replace it with a new one. This is a skill I will hone over time and with practice.

When I have learned to love and trust myself again, I have, in effect, granted myself the ultimate freedom: the freedom to have nothing hidden. There is still plenty to explore both inside my head and outside in the world. The difference is that I *welcome* newness rather than *resist* it. I have pulled my need for alcohol up by the roots, not just trimmed the branches. I have moved to a new mental and spiritual environment, planted a new seed, and have grown new roots. They deepen with the days. I no longer expect anything except what is received. My greatest thought is to achieve a measure of peace, to be at peace with the way things are. I recognize that

I possess the skills to change myself, and I can if I want. In the meantime, I will be working on being peace-filled.

I can live in my world, loving you and setting you free, all in the same moment. I can resonate with love and light, and you can notice or you can not notice. Either way, it does not change me. Just because another person does not see something in me, does not mean it is not there. When they see it in themselves, they will see it in me. When I see it in myself, I will see it in them. Nothing happens outside first. It all comes from within. I go within to find the solution. When I experience pain, it is because of the way I see the situation. The situation does not have power over me. I am bigger than the perceived issue.

It is a benevolent gift to understand one's thinking, an accomplishment to perceive with clarity one's own mind.

Like an autumn leaf fluttering from a tree, I need not try to climb back up. I am done being a leaf. It is okay that I fall. It is time to fall. The breeze carries me to the stream. I float. It is wet, and I am away from all that is familiar. I am pushed to the banks. It is there that I eventually deteriorate. I die so that I can nourish another and once again become something new. I need not fight the way things are. Rather, I accept what is.

In one of my yesterdays, I made a choice, a decision. I stayed dedicated. It has effected all my tomorrows. May you now make a choice that will effect all of your tomorrows. Whoever you are being today, I hope you are learning to trust yourself. It is then that you will be learning to love yourself.

Dialogue 7

November 2010: Sobriety—Day 2,472
A: *Can this be my life? I am so happy that this is my life!*

B: *Yes, yes, you are.*

A: *It's better than I thought.*

B: *You limited your thinking while you were drinking.*

A: *Yes, I did. And even for some time after.*

B: *So many things are possible now.*

A: *Yes.*

B: *The darkness is not gone, however.*

A: *That's okay. I understand why it is there. I see the necessity. It can be there. It needn't bother me, and if it does, I will come to you.*

B: *I know. Of this I am certain.*

About the Author

Lisa Neumann is a life skill and recovery coach, Certified ThetaHealer™, and a fully recovered alcoholic. She is the founder of Competency Coaching: Life Skill & Recovery Coaching, a creative coaching agency that works with individuals who struggle with sustaining sobriety. She lives with her family in San Juan Capistrano, California.

Appendix A

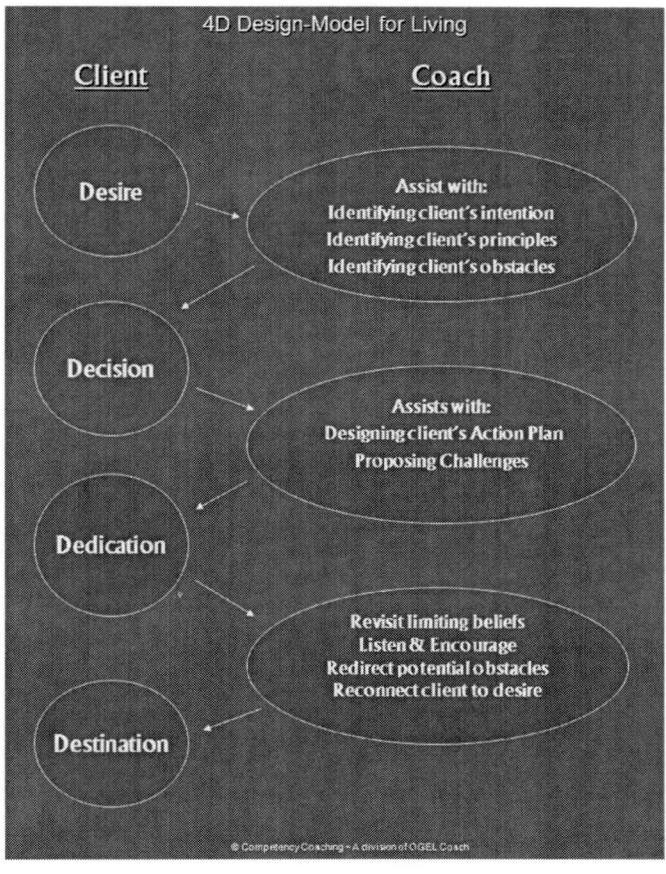

Resources

Competency Coaching: Coaching for the Addictive Mind
www.CompetencyCoaching.com

The Art of Sobriety
www.TheArtOfSobriety.com

Lisa Neumann, founder
Life Skill & Recovery Coaching
Certified ThetaHealer™
San Juan Capistrano, California, USA
(949) 240-7736

Specialties:
• One-on-one recovery coaching and group coaching
• Living the Five Key Competencies Workshop
• How to Apply Universal Principles Workshop
• The Art of Sobriety: Inner Light Recovery Workshop (3-Day Intensive)
• "Why" Workshop for families and friends of addicts

My Voice of Truth Coaching
www.MyVoiceOfTruthCoaching.com

Stephanie Gagos, founder and life coach
Nyack, New York, USA
(914) 419-8323

Specialties:
• Childhood trauma and abuse coaching
• One-on-one coaching, group coaching, and workshops

CoachA
www.CoachA.net

Christine H. Andersen, founder and life coach
Dubai, United Arab Emirates

Specialties:
• Body image and food addiction
• One-on-one coaching with focus on weight, addiction, and
  confidence-building

Alicia McNaughton
www.SeatOfTheSoulMassage.com
www.AliciaMcNaughton.MassagePlanet.com

Certified Holistic Healer and Lightworker
Seat of the Soul Massage
Laguna Hills, California, USA
(714) 625-5457

Specialties:
• Awakenings
• Reiki
• Readings
• The Art of Sobriety: Inner Light Recovery Workshop (3-Day Intensive)

Michelle Conboy, MA
www.RelationshipCafe.net
www.RelationshipCafe.net/PrivateRelationshipMentoring

Relationship Expert
Founder of Relationship Café
Laguna Hills, California, USA
(949) 553-6100

Specialties:
Women's mentor in relationship and intimacy, financial empowerment, and work that makes a difference

Organizations:
Alcoholics Anonymous www.AA.org

Narcotics Anonymous www.NA.org

Pills Anonymous www.PillsAnonymous.org

The Tapping Solution
Nick Ortner
Meridian Tapping (EFT) www.TheTappingSolution.com

The Work of Byron Katie®
Self-inquiry www.TheWork.com

Foundation for Inner Peace
Publisher of *A Course in Miracles*: a self-study spiritual-thought system that teaches the way to universal love through forgiveness www.acim.org

ThetaHealing™
www.ThetaHealing.com www.ThetaHealingLA.com

Suggested Reading

Allen, James. *As a Man Thinketh.*

Bartlett, DC, Richard. *Matrix Energetics: The Science and Art of Transformation.*

Bradden, Gregg. *Fractal Time: The Secret of 2012 and a New World Age.*

Bradden, Gregg. *The Divine Matrix: Bridging Time, Space, Miracles, and Belief.*

Bradden, Gregg. *Secrets of the Lost Mode of Prayer: The Hidden Power of Beauty, Blessing, Wisdom and Hurt.*

Bradden, Gregg. *The Spontaneous Healing of Belief: Shattering the Paradigm of False Limits.*

Capra, Fritjof. *The Tao of Physics.*

Carter-Scott, PhD, Cherie. *If Life Is a Game, These Are the Rules.*

Cole, K. C. *First You Build a Cloud: And Other Reflections on Physics as a Way of Life.*

Covey, Stephen R. *The 7 Habits of Highly Effective People.*

Covey, Stephen M. R. *The Speed of Trust.*

Genz, Henning. *Nothingness: The Science of Empty Space.*

Katie, Byron, with Stephen Mitchell. *A Thousand Names for Joy: Living in Harmony with the Way Things Are.*

Katie, Byron, with Stephen Mitchell. *Loving What Is: Four Questions That Can Change Your Life.*

Kelley, Tim. *True Purpose: 12 Strategies for Discovering the Difference You Are Meant to Make.*

Kurtz, Ernest, and Katherine Ketcham. *The Spirituality of Imperfection: Storytelling and the Search for Meaning.*

Lederman, Leon, with Teresi. *The God Particle: If the Universe Is the Answer, What Is the Question?*

Lipton, Bruce. *The Biology of Belief.*

Lipton, Bruce, and Steve Bhaerman. *Spontaneous Evolution: Our Positive Future (And a Way to Get There from Here).*

McTaggart, Lynne. *The Field: The Quest for the Secret Force of the Universe.*

Milanovich, Norma, and Shirley McCune. *The Light Shall Set You Free.*

Naparstek, Belleruth. *Your Sixth Sense: Unlocking the Power of Your Intuition.*

Needleman, Jacob. *Why Can't We Be Good?*

Phillips, Brent. *Where Science Meets Spirit: The Formula for Miracles.*

Stribal, Vianna. *Theta Healing.*

Stribal, Vianna. *Advanced Theta Healing.*

Walsch, Neale Donald. *Conversations with God.*

Walsch, Neale Donald. *Friendship with God.*

Wauters, Ambika. *The Book of Chakras: Discover the Hidden Forces within You.*

Williamson, Marianne. *The Age of Miracles: Embracing the New Midlife.*

Williamson, Marianne. *The Gift of Change: Spiritual Guidance for Living Your Best Life.*

Notes

Part I: The Observation

[1]   Bruce H. Lipton, PhD and Steve Bhaerman, *Spontaneous Evolution: Our Positive Future (And a Way to Get There from Here)* (New York City: Hay House, Inc., 2009), xxii.

Part II: The Process

[1]   Lipton and Bhaerman, *Spontaneous Evolution: Our Positive Future (And a Way to Get There from Here)*, 34.

[2]   Ibid., 103.

Part III: The Essentials

[1]   Bruce H. Lipton, PhD, *The Biology of Belief: Unleashing the Power of Consciousness, Matter & Miracles* (New York City: Hay House, Inc., 2008), 68.

[2]   ThinkQuest.com, 2010 http://library.thinkquest.org/3487/qp.html, accessed October 22, 2010.

[3]   Lynne McTaggart, *The Field: The Quest for the Secret of the Universe* (New York City: Harper, 2008), Prologue XXXVII.

[4]   Ibid.

[5]   Lipton and Bhaerman, *Spontaneous Evolution: Our Positive Future (And a Way to Get There from Here)*, 101.

[6]   Ibid., 31.

7   Lipton, *The Biology of Belief: Unleashing the Power of Consciousness, Matter &
    Miracles*, 136.

8   Lipton and Bhaerman, *Spontaneous Evolution: Our Positive Future (And a
    Way to Get There from Here)*, 34.

9   Lipton, *The Biology of Belief: Unleashing the Power of Consciousness, Matter &
    Miracles*, 34.

10 Ambika Wauters, *The Book of Chakras: Discover the Hidden Forces within You*
    (New York: Barron's Educational Series, Inc., 2002), 16.

11 Brent Phillips, *Where Science Meets Spirit: The Formula for Miracles* (Phillips,
    2010), 45.

12 Lipton, *The Biology of Belief: Unleashing the Power of Consciousness, Matter
    & Miracles*, 7.

13 Wikipedia.org, 2010 http://en.wikipedia.org/wiki/Thomas_Edison, accessed
    August 14, 2010.

Part IV: The Competencies

1   *Merriam-Webster Dictionary*, 11th Edition, 46.

2   Dictionary.com, 2010 http://dictionary.reference.com/browse/competence,
    accessed September 30, 2010.

3   Byron Katie with Stephen Mitchell, *A Thousand Names for Joy: Living in
    Harmony with the Way Things Are* (New York: Three Rivers Press, 2007), 142.

Part VI: The Partnership

1   Encyclopedia Britannica.com 2010. http://www.britannica.com/EBchecked/
    topic/406283/natural-law, accessed August 8, 2010.

2   Albert Einstein. BrainyQuote.com, Xplore Inc, 2011. http://www.
    brainyquote.com/quotes/quotes/a/alberteins133991.html, accessed January
    13, 2011.

3   Socrates. BrainyQuote.com, Xplore Inc, 2011. http://www.brainyquote.
    com/quotes/authors/s/socrates_2.html, accessed July 14, 2011.

Lightning Source UK Ltd.
Milton Keynes UK
UKOW04n0059131015

260418UK00007B/99/P